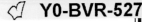
The Business of

Same Day Deliveries

Financial systems and operational practices designed to increase profits for small businesses

By

JIM HANSELL

Although the author and publisher have made every effort to ensure the accuracy and completeness of information contained in this book, we assume no responsibility for errors, inaccuracies, omissions, or any inconsistency herein. Any slights of people, places, or organizations are unintentional.

Library of Congress Cataloging-in-Publication Data
Hansell, James M.
   The Business of Same Day Deliveries: financial systems and operational practices designed to increase profits for small businesses / James M. Hansell. — 1st ed.
      p.cm.
   Includes bibliographical references and index.

Library of Congress Control Number: 2005929402

ISBN 09770161-0-2

   1. Business I. Hansell, Jim. II. Title.

Published in the United States
MCD Publishing, a division of Hansell Corporation
P.O. Box 330, Santa Clara, CA 95052

Preface

The idea for this book was not something that happened overnight. It germinated for a couple of years after I joined a Bay Area group of couriers that had banded together for political clout under the name of the Association of Messengers and Couriers of California. As I began to attend the quarterly meetings of AMCS (now called the California Delivery Association), I became aware of a certain hesitancy by members to share information. That was natural because each member company could potentially take any other member's business.

A year or two later, a local CPA who handled financial matters for some of the members gave a talk at a well-attended meeting, where he discussed budgeting, forecasting, and other financial topics. One concept he mentioned was the need to create an industry-specific chart of accounts. While his talk was more academic than practical, I could see from the questions posed to him that this group of business owners and managers needed answers to a number of financial and operational issues. I could also see that they preferred to share current practices with and obtain information from someone who was not a potential competitor. It was at this meeting that I decided to begin to accumulate data and document experiences that would benefit anyone in the delivery business.

Over the years, I had garnered a deep understanding of issues related to managing a company in this industry. But it seemed to me that because of my financial education and experience, the most useful information I could share with other small business managers was related to financial systems, reports, and controls. Accordingly, this book is written from the standpoint of simple financial systems and reports that should be installed in any small business that wants to enhance its profits.

I consider myself a financial expert; my qualifications are as follows. My undergraduate degree in accounting was followed by an MBA. The first seven years of my work experience occurred on the audit staff of Price Waterhouse & Co., where I obtained first-hand knowledge of how some of the largest clients in the San Francisco office managed their businesses through their financial systems. In addition, I was selected to help form the firm's small business group, where I dealt with a number of successful small firms and saw how good financial systems contributed to their success. My next twenty years were spent primarily in senior financial management positions (controller or vice president finance) in the Silicon Valley high tech industry. There, I installed my own financial systems and controls in a handful of companies, both large and small, private and public. After buying Mid-Counties Delivery Service in early 1988, I attempted to work with the financial system that had been installed by the previous owner. However, this system did not provide me with the information I needed to ensure that the company's prices were adequate, that each driver was producing an acceptable level of gross margin, or that the company was capable of providing the returns I expected from my investment. I then began the process of building the financial structure and reports that are the primary topic of this book.

As the chapters of this book began to grow, my experiences as an owner/manager of a company in the transportation industry allowed me to cover topics that I might not have been willing to discuss with competitors if I had still been in the business. I have often mentioned the name of my former company, Mid-Counties Delivery Service, and described the way we did things there. The readers should know that I do not hold Mid-Counties up as a model for the way business should be conducted in this industry. It was simply the vehicle from which I operated, learned, experimented, succeeded and in some cases failed during the 15 years I served my customers. However, this book has almost nothing to do with Mid-Counties, but has everything to do with the combination of practices and experiences that have proven to lead to increased profitability and success in the delivery business.

Foreword

This book addresses profitability, operating issues, reports and systems for the thousands of small, same day delivery businesses that make up a significant portion of the delivery industry. Although the concepts and issues discussed herein are mentioned in terms specific to this industry, they apply to almost all of the approximately 25 million small businesses in the United States that provide half of U.S. employment and approximately 75 percent of new jobs.

I have been interested in the risk-reward concept of business since I was very young. But it was not until I bought Mid-Counties Delivery Service and gained first-hand knowledge about how the cards were stacked against small businesses that I became a great admirer of how these businesses survive against significant odds. Certainly it is true that the bigger a business is, the more power it has and the more likely it is to cause change to make itself more successful. Global oil companies are free to increase their prices daily; insurance companies are constantly increasing medical insurance and workers' compensation rates - with the approval of state insurance departments; mammoth drug companies sell medicines blessed by the Federal Drug Administration that are harmful to consumers; and the world's largest retailer, Wal-Mart, in its quest to obtain ever lower costs and higher margins, has directed the transfer of much manufacturing to China. This transfer by a single company has permanently eliminated thousands of manufacturing jobs from the U. S. workforce, and apparently has also caused the closure of a number U. S. companies - large and small.

Small businesses, on the other hand, are almost never able to cause change in the marketplace for their betterment; they must survive on hard work, commitment to their customers, willingness to change, and the intelligence of their managements.

I am convinced that most small businesses operate under the principles of honesty, commitment, and respect. Most managements would affirm that these principles must apply to all parties with an interest in the success of the business - customers, creditors, employees and owners. But as companies grow or shrink, as operating conditions change and as competition arises, the application of these principles is not always the same to each of the interested parties.

Most managements associate business success with ever-increasing revenues and profits and happy customers. Sometimes, however, customer satisfaction or profitability comes at the expense of another of the interested parties. While this group is more often than not the employees of a company, in some cases, as shown by Wal-Mart, it can also be a company's vendors. In the delivery industry, happy customers seem to migrate to businesses that provide economical services through employees that are committed to consistently provide these services, even under difficult or changing circumstances.

Providing economical services requires a tight control over costs. In the delivery industry, this means that employees must be at work on time, absenteeism is controlled, drivers stick to their routes and schedules, vehicles are kept in good working condition, and appropriate support software and hardware is used to provide delivery status. Accordingly, systems to control, segregate and measure costs are vitally important to the success of a business of any size.

For some customers, satisfactory completion of a job is not enough. They often need to know in-transit status or want proof of delivery times as well as acceptance signatures, since they often lose packages that have been delivered to them. These additional services come with additional costs that usually cannot be passed on to the customers.

Sometimes the need to maintain or lower rates while increasing services pits employees against customers in managements' eyes. When revenues do not provide adequate margins, managements must look to cost reductions, and many times those reductions come out of the pockets of employees. There can be a fine line between cost containment and creative employment practices where employees can provide almost as large a part of a company's gross margins as do the customers.

In California, and I suspect in other parts of the country, an example of this type of cost avoidance is currently being attempted by many companies because of the condition of the workers' compensation program. When governments foolishly let statutory costs increase out of control, creative managements must devise new ways of acquiring these services that will eliminate or contain the skyrocketing costs. Hence, many companies in the delivery industry are reclassifying employees to owner/operator status (independent contractors). The independent contractor classification readily lends itself to relief from certain other statutory costs, such as overtime and payroll tax rates. However, the real benefit to using independent contractors is that businesses are not required to carry workers' compensation on them — and California has typically had the highest workers' compensation rates in the country.

However, many more issues other than workers' compensation affect the survival of small businesses. Many of these concern costs such as minimum wage rates, overtime calculations, "living wage rates" assessed by individual cities, medical insurance rates, etc., that are outside the control of the small business. But what is under the control of the small business is the system to identify and manage every expenditure, to make sure that an appropriate value is received for all monies spent, and to make sure that the assets of the company (including the employees) are providing a reasonable return. And in order to do this, it is imperative that small businesses put in place the same type of systems used by large businesses to maximize their margins. The identification of these systems for small companies is the purpose of this book.

Dedicated to my loving wife Kathleen,
for her support of my many ventures over the years,
and my children Sara and James who contributed to the
growth and success of Mid-Counties Delivery Service.

Table of Contents

Same Day Deliveries | 1 |

S ame day deliveries constitute a small, niche service area in the large transportation industry. It is not well known or understood by consumers or even by most people in other parts of the transportation business. Initially, this market was served by what historically had been called messengers. Later, the messengers came to be called couriers as the need to deliver messages died out and the materials to be delivered became much larger.

What is a Same Day Delivery?

The distinction of the same day market is that pickup and delivery occur on the same calendar day. Although pickups and deliveries can occur any time during the 24-hour period from midnight to midnight, most of the work is handled between 7:00 am and 7:00 pm because most of it is done for businesses.

Same day deliveries have been available for as long as people have needed to send urgent messages and materials. An early example is the Olympic marathon, supposedly based on the distance a runner traveled to make a same day delivery of a message from the Plain of Marathon to Athens about the status of a battle between the Greeks and Persians.

Although same day deliveries can be made nationally and in some cases even internationally, the short time between pickup and delivery has essentially limited this market to local and regional deliveries. The short time between pickup and delivery is the defining difference between same day work and next day or slower deliveries. A company gets almost no efficiencies of scale in the same day market, and, of course, the concept of consolidation at hubs, critical to the success of the overnight business, is not applicable.

Types of Same Day Deliveries

Same day work is divided into two categories. The first is for unscheduled work; these are typically called on-demand or on-call deliveries. The second category is for scheduled, repetitive deliveries; this work is called routed deliveries. Neither of these types of deliveries lends itself well to consolidation, although routed work certainly provides a much greater opportunity for combining deliveries than on-demand does.

Market Entry

Same day deliveries can be made by birds, dogs, dolphins, foot couriers, bike messengers, taxis, couriers in cars and pickups with camper shells, vans, cargo vans, bob-tails and straight trucks, tractor-trailers, helicopters, scheduled commercial airlines, and chartered airplanes and jets. Since it is easy to enter this market with little investment and no training, a continuous stream of new companies enters and exits the market. The overnight market is more difficult to enter because the freight must be stored overnight and a higher driver headcount is usually required, since it is unlikely that the driver who made the pickup will make the delivery.

Market Growth and Size

While same day work over the last twenty years has lost volume to fax machines and the Internet, overall it has grown in line with the explosive growth of the overnight business handled by Federal Express, DHL, UPS, Airborne, and the US Postal Service. As businesses and individuals became increasingly accustomed to faxing and overnighting documents, a corresponding surge in same day business occurred. This growth came mainly from on-demand deliveries because people had become accustomed to immediate deliveries by fax machines as well as morning deliveries of overnight shipments. The urgent distribution of parts, computer equipment, medical supplies, and even heavy freight, has driven many couriers and truckers into the warehousing business, which in turn has fed same day deliveries.

Of other reasons for the increase in on-demand shipments, one of the most important has been the implementation of just-in-time inventory systems by businesses that maintain inventories or manufacture products. While reducing the size and carrying values of inventories around the world, just-in-time procurement has resulted in shortages of products, parts, and subassemblies caused by mistakes and errors, which has been a major boon to the same day delivery business.

Another significant reason has been the growth in shipping perishables. Numerous companies now do nothing but ship blood and body parts, various food products, flowers, and even meals.

These three reasons have been the main causes of the major increase in same day deliveries over the past decade. It is my opinion that routed work has not increased much over this period, especially for couriers. The major portion of outsourced routed work seems to go to truckers, because much of the work tends to be for heavy, large loads. One of the largest classes of same day work for truckers is pickups from and deliveries to freight forwarders. Since most freight forwarders do not have their own vehicles and drivers, some trucking companies have become quite large working only for the freight forwarders. Courier pricing tends to be based on lighter loads that do not lend themselves to consolidation and as a result, much of the courier-routed work comes from financial institutions — banks, credit unions, title companies, payroll services, etc.

By far the largest part of the same day market is not outsourced to independent carriers, but is handled by businesses that use their employees and vehicles to deliver their own products. These in-house deliveries tend to be the most cost effective when unusual or very specific delivery times are involved or when special equipment must be used. Also, unless the company making the delivery is able to charge for it, or its customer pays, the product being delivered must have a fairly high gross margin; otherwise, in-house deliveries are generally not cost-efficient and the work is outsourced to truckers or couriers, that are generally less expensive on a "per delivery basis" than in-house deliveries. The point is that it is easy for the delivery cost to be more than the profit from the sale of the product being delivered.

Not long ago, Webvan was formed, with the expectation that it would become the largest same day delivery service in the world. How Webvan was able to raise as much money as it did to make free same day deliveries of groceries within a radius of 100 miles of its warehouses was a complete mystery to anyone in the delivery business. The cost of making the deliveries was so much more than the pretax margins provided by the groceries that everyone except investors and Wall Street financiers knew that Webvan would have to increase its delivery charges, or it would not stay in business. And, of course, it did not. Webvan proved that if you undercharge or give away a service that should be charged for, you could quickly build a very large-volume business. Had Webvan's groceries provided enough margin, or had they charged a fair price for the delivery, this company would probably still be around.

Under pricing is a general problem in the same day delivery business. The for-hire portion of the market is made up of thousands of small truckers and couriers. These small businesses tend to price their services under the prices charged by their larger competitors, which keeps profits low and limits growth potential.

In the same day business, most companies have revenues of under $500,000 per year. Companies with annual revenues of $500,000 to $2.5 million are considered mid-size, and those over $2.5 million are considered big. Except in the large metropolitan areas, it is rare to find a same day delivery company with annual revenues of more than $10 million.

I have never seen a published report of the total market size for same day deliveries, but I would guess it is small, probably less than $5 billion a year. This revenue number is produced by thousands of little businesses. While the companies are as diverse as the niches they serve, they have several things in common. They tend to have a close, almost personal relationship with their customers, and they provide very competitive rates. Because the same day market is small, fragmented, and difficult to manage, no company has been able to get to even $100 million in sales, to the best of my knowledge. A number of people thought the Internet would provide an efficient method of taking orders and scheduling deliveries around the country and internationally, enabling a few large same day companies to develop, but to date that has not happened. Even during the 1990s' roll-up mania, the handful of large, public, same day companies that were created have mostly disappeared. The one or two that have survived are still relatively small, certainly under $100 million in revenue.

The overnight market, on the other hand, is quite a bit larger, probably close to $250 billion a year. This market is well served by a handful of large multinational players, and (other than the consolidation occurring from the actions of the German post office) there probably will not be any new major players in the overnight market.

All the overnight companies now offer same day deliveries, but they farm the work out to couriers and local truckers because it is very disruptive to their own routes. They price this work to include their overhead structure, which makes each delivery extremely expensive.

Same Day Deliveries Versus Overnight Deliveries

The differences between the same day market and the markets for deferred deliveries are significant. They have made it almost impossible for the overnight and other deferred delivery companies to participate in the same day market. On the other hand, most same day companies are able to generate up to 50 percent of their revenues by making local deferred deliveries.

A few of the most significant differences in these markets are:

Same Day Deliveries	Vs.	Overnight and Slower Deliveries
No inventory of work is waiting to be delivered at the start of each workday.		All of yesterday's pickups are awaiting delivery each morning.
Pickup requests have designated delivery times. For couriers, they are usually within 1-2 hours of pickup, within 3-5 hours of pickup, and over 5 hours after pickup. For truckers, same day deliveries are called "specials," usually within 4 hours of receiving the call, or "standard," as agreed, but usually within normal working hours (before 6 p.m.).		One driver is assigned to a specific area and typically makes deliveries during the morning. Pickups are made by that same driver in the same area in the afternoon
Ordinarily, the driver who makes the pickup also makes the delivery.		The driver who makes the pickup almost never makes the delivery.
Couriers: Because there is such a short time between pickup and delivery, there is little chance of combining deliveries to share costs. Each delivery must be priced to be profitable on its own. Truckers: Usually have more than 5 hours after pickup to make their deliveries, and therefore have a better chance of combining several pickups into one delivery.		The base-deferred delivery price is usually less than the base same day delivery price.

Growing a Delivery Business $\big|2\big|$

Subjects covered in this chapter
- *Activities designed to increase sales*
- *Benefits of purchasing revenue*

W hen I purchased Mid-Counties Delivery Service in the late 1980s, the company had grown 100 percent the year before, without a sales person. This doubling in size mistakenly led me to believe that the company's sales would continue to increase because of its location, high level of service, or pricing structure. For the first few years, I did not employ a sales person. We did obtain a certain level of new business, but because of the normal losses of existing business (customers' being bought and moving out of the area, going out of business, or using their own employees for deliveries), our overall growth was not acceptable. I attempted to devote about a third of my time to drumming up new business, but time-consuming crises seemed to occur regularly, and my sales activities were not particularly productive.

Advertising

Yellow Page Ads
At the time I bought Mid-Counties, the previous owner believed that yellow page ads were necessary to acquire new customers, and he recommended I increase this type of advertising if I wanted the business to grow outside the original area. I followed his advice and significantly increased the number and size of our ads for the areas where we had most of our activities. I also began running yellow page ads in adjacent areas where I wanted to develop a presence. While the yellow page ads I contracted for were affordable at the time, as years went by I found that their cost increased faster than the company's revenues; what had been an

affordable tool to stimulate interest in our services became a heavy burden during the early 90s when California was in a recession.

I find several problems with yellow page ads. First, it is often difficult to ascertain what portion of new business comes from the ads. The yellow page sales reps always say that it is easy to tell which new customers learned about your service through the yellow pages by simply asking them. However, I found over the years that the person calling to establish a new account had simply been told to do so and had no idea how the person who made the decision learned about us.

Another significant problem with yellow page ads is that a business must contract with the publisher for as long as 18 months into the future for the ads. If business revenues drop, there is no way to get out from under high, fixed monthly payments for ads that might still require a year or more of payments. For example, in the early 90s, the Loma Prieta earthquake was centered a few miles from our office. This earthquake destroyed many of the roads we used to make our deliveries and many of our small customers went out of business. It took almost a year for the infrastructure to be rebuilt and for us to return to our previous level of operations. Our yellow page ads were very costly during the months after the earthquake, but had no value to us. This was when I began to cut back on many of the ads. In summary, when business is good and growing, owners tend not to think or do much about yellow page ads. And when business is tough and slowing, the yellow page contract requires a fixed payment, and the owner is unable to cut the ads back to an appropriate level.

During the final years I owned Mid-Counties, I had reduced my yellow page advertising and ran only small ads where I already had a significant level of business. I did, however, keep one large color ad in the local phone book. This ad was slanted toward pushing our domestic and international airfreight capabilities. Although we received very few calls for courier and trucking services due to the yellow page ads, we received a large number of calls for freight forwarding. These calls were easy to track because they were from businesses that did not have accounts with us; each call was ordinarily paid for in cash and the amounts were much greater than any incidental calls for same day local ground deliveries (see page 83 for our policy of requiring cash for the first order from all new accounts). A large shipment by air could easily be $1,000 and could be more than $5,000. I loved seeing all this cash activity, and so I knew the yellow page ads for airfreight were very successful where the ads we ran over many years for ground services did not come close to paying for themselves.

The terrorist attack on September 11, 2001 slammed the door on air shipments for months, but had much less effect on our operations than the Loma Prieta earthquake because the cost of our yellow page ads in 2001 was so much lower that it was not a major concern.

Brochures

Another favorite type of advertising is a company brochure. Professionally designed and printed brochures can be very expensive, but they are generally well liked by sales people since they are attractive handouts during sales calls. However, it is even more difficult to judge the value of brochures than yellow page ads. At Mid-Counties, we always seemed to need new brochures because our business was changing, and yet we still had a large supply of old ones on hand. We finally stopped having them printed outside, and, as we did for new rate sheets, either printed them in house using Microsoft Excel or created them in house and took them to a low-cost copy service like Kinko's for multicolor printing.

Signage on Vehicles

Signage on trucks can also be very expensive, but it seemed to be important to many of our customers, just as uniforms on drivers were important to certain customers. At Mid-Counties, we had large, distinct and attractively colored signs on our vehicles. These signs, which were centered around our logo, included a description of some of our services or of geographical areas we covered.

We did get a few calls over the years because of the advertising information on our trucks, but we received many more calls from irate automobile drivers calling on their cell phones to complain about our drivers. It was easy to make such a call when our 800 telephone number was conveniently displayed. I found that if we received several such calls in one day about a specific driver, this person was often involved in an accident. We therefore began to discipline or sometimes discharge drivers on whom we received these calls.

The Company Website

Almost all small businesses now have an informative website. For delivery companies, many websites are tied to the company's operating system so that customers can place orders without talking to a customer service person. Later, the customer can access the system to determine delivery status. However, aside from order entry and proof-of-delivery features, practically all new customers will go to a company's website to learn more about the company, and this provides a level of credibility. If the information is presented in a professional manner, the site can be one of the most influential forms of advertising available to a business. Also, many internet search engines need to be able to provide users with information about local services and their capabilities. This is a very good source of new business for any delivery service with a web site.

Direct Sales

After three years of sub-par revenue growth at Mid-Counties, I finally faced the fact that in order to grow, we needed a full-time, experienced sales person completely dedicated to this activity. I employed a sales manager, who almost immediately began to bring in a steady stream of new business.

Shortly after joining the company, the new sales manager identified some employee actions that were not conducive to good customer service and were resulting in missed revenues. I learned that operations was making decisions about accepting, declining, or postponing work based on their own scheduling problems. While a certain amount of this is to be expected for a small company in the on-demand delivery business, over the long run a delivery company must meet the needs of its customers or get out of that segment of the market. It is not a good idea to bring customers into a company's scheduling and driver problems. I found that operations would turn down business from some of our best customers rather than instruct some drivers to work overtime, and then tell the customer we could not do the work because the driver was involved in an accident or had an emergency at home. Also, there were times operations would decline business requested early in the day for long runs because they assumed we would be busy later that day and did not want drivers sent out of the area.

In addition to bringing in new customers and new business, the sales manager balanced our management team. Instead of having our decisions solely based on input from operations and finance, we began getting input from the sales side of the business, which meant that our customers finally had a voice.

As business increased from our sales program, I began to consider several other alternatives to increase growth.

Expansion of Service Area

Since we were easily the most dominant local ground service in our geographic area (we had the greatest revenues and the most drivers), I was certain our growth rate would drop or level off if we did not expand beyond our traditional service area. We opened a San Jose facility so we would be closer to our customers there. We supported this facility for about five years, but I finally concluded that a remote location without on-site management is expensive and difficult to manage, and without dedicated local sales activity it does not contribute much to increased customer satisfaction or sales growth.

Expansion of Services Offered

We had always considered ourselves an on-demand delivery service. But our vehicles had continually increased in size as we were asked to move larger loads, and I began to consider other markets that required large vehicles, such as hauling air cargo for the freight forwarders. Many local freight forwarders did not have their own vehicles, and most of those that did would not send them "over the hill" to Santa Cruz and points south.

Revenue Growth Produced Internally and Revenue Purchased

While the freight-forwarding market was developing for us, I began to consider buying a courier or delivery business in our service area that would fit in with our type of deliveries. I developed a model, the key elements of which were:

- The business of the acquired company should not be completely dissimilar from the Mid-Counties business and should contribute to the use of our specific vehicle fleet.

- The acquired company should provide a gross margin of at least 20 to 25 percent (revenues less direct costs).

- The business of the acquired company should fit well with the Mid-Counties operating software.

- The order taking, order entry, pricing, and billing should be transferable to the Mid-Counties customer service group with limited systems changes.

- The acquired company should not require extensive asset purchases.

- Ideally, the acquired company should operate out of its current location, taking into account that a few Mid-Counties large vehicles would probably be transferred to the new company.

- Certain operations and sales personnel from the acquired company would join Mid-Counties.

- An added benefit could be a service offered by the acquired company not offered by Mid-Counties, which we could begin to offer to our existing customers.

The benefit to Mid-Counties from a compatible purchase would be that most of the gross margin from the acquired company's sales would fall to our bottom line to pay for it. I was not interested in a purchase where we would have to replace their drivers or decrease their driver pay in order to achieve the desired gross margins. And I certainly was not interested in a purchase where we picked up a lot of low margin business and had to significantly increase the rates to the acquired company's customers and hope that they stayed with us.

One of the freight forwarders we did work for was a one-man operation we had sublet space from in San Jose. This small freight forwarder handled the airfreight for a small number of Santa Cruz companies that were also Mid-Counties customers. As our relationship grew, he gave up his office in San Jose, sublet space from Mid-Counties, and moved his office to our facility in Santa Cruz. His revenue was about one half of ours, but his sales came from only a handful of customers. This concentration of business in so few customers played havoc with his cash flow. He was interested in folding his business into ours and becoming the manager of our freight forwarding division (we were already doing about $100,000 a year in freight forwarding), and assuming the responsibility of growing this division into a significant freight forwarding business serving the South Bay. We worked out an agreement to buy his business and pay him off over three years, and he joined Mid-Counties. Since his background was in sales and since Mid-Counties had excess delivery capacity, it seemed like a perfect match.

The business we purchased, in addition to normal freight forwarding, also did a fair amount of specialized mail distribution called "international remail". This service was for lightweight advertising matter such as envelopes or catalogs that were shipped out of the U.S. to foreign destinations. The competition for this service was the U.S. Postal service as well as Federal Express, DHL, and UPS. We either sent the material to specific countries and had the material distributed through the postal service of that country, or we arranged for the deliveries in the foreign countries. As in most of our other services, our niche was faster, more reliable service.

Although we encountered a number of problems with the merger of the freight forwarding operation into Mid-Counties, our overall strategy worked well, and by September 11, 2001, when the industry permanently changed, our freight forwarding division (operated under the name of MCD Air) had become larger than the Mid-Counties ground division and was growing much faster.

By this time, I had seen the benefits and potential of buying established companies to supplement internal growth. I had developed a set of requirements that I considered mandatory to make a purchase successful, and I had worked through a major merger of dissimilar entities. I also identified several other ground services that appeared to fit the Mid-Counties acquisition criteria (unfortunately, most delivery companies do not record their financial statements in such a manner that one can readily see their gross margin on sales). But I was faced with a difficult decision. Should I continue to build Mid-Counties by purchasing additional transportation businesses and assuming large debt loads, even though most of our customers were seeing their revenues decrease in line with the slow-down in the economy. Ultimately, I decided to wait until our revenues again began to increase before undertaking another acquisition.

Profitability and Managing by the Numbers

3

Subjects covered in this chapter
- *Standard financial statements*
- *Automating financial statement preparation*
- *An easy-to-understand chart of accounts*
- *Different income statement formats for different audiences*
- *Examples of departmental reporting*
- *Profit center accounting*

All businesses, big and small, should have a financial system that tracks each detail of revenue and cost, summarizes items by functional classification, and rolls up into operating statements that are simple to read, brief and pinpoint profitability by each profit center. The system must provide information for income tax reporting, as well as for various interested parties outside the company such as vendors, banks and other lenders, and credit rating companies such as Dun & Bradstreet. The same system should provide the details that management needs to run the company profitably. Although this information should all come from the same basic data, the reports will be in different formats for different users. Dun & Bradstreet or vendors do not need the same level of detail that operating management does.

The formal names of the three most important statements that must result from a company's financial system are the **balance sheet,** the **income statement** (or statement of operations), and the **statement of cash flow.** Of the three statements, the income statement is the most important one to management, since it has the information needed to manage the profitability of a company.

Balance Sheets

Balance sheets are pretty much the same for all service companies: they start with cash and end with retained earnings. Balance sheets are used primarily as an indication of credit-worthiness and are of particular interest to lenders, such as banks and leasing/ financing companies.. Certain key ratios are related to balance sheet accounts that management should strive to maintain, as listed on page 48.

Balance sheets follow the same format for all service companies. The assets of the company are listed first, followed by liabilities and owners' equity. Assets less liabilities equals owners' equity— hence the term "balance sheet." The detailed assets and liabilities should be listed in a specific order. Cash on hand (petty cash) is listed first, followed by cash in banks, cash in savings accounts, and then in order by the other assets that are the closest to becoming cash. All assets that will convert to cash during one operating cycle of the business (not to exceed one year) are called **current assets.** For a delivery company, other current assets besides cash include trade accounts receivable followed by prepaid expenses and operating supplies.

Assets listed below current assets will not be converted to cash within one operating period, but should still be listed in order of their probability of becoming cash. Examples of these **non-current assets** include notes receivable, depreciable assets (vehicles, office equipment, etc.), deposits such as the last month's rent, and finally assets that will not be converted for a very long period of time such as goodwill, investments in other companies, or land.

The listing of liabilities follows the same logic as assets, with the liabilities required to be paid first listed first. This means that if a company pays its employees every two weeks and its accounts payable after thirty days, then accrued payrolls should be listed before trade payables. Liabilities that will be paid within one year are labeled **current liabilities** and should include the principal portion of notes and contracts payable that will be paid over the next twelve months. If a company charges interest on past due accounts and if it finds that many accounts refuse to pay the interest charge, then it is better to record these interest charges as "deferred revenue" near the end of current liabilities. As these charges are paid, they should be moved to Interest Income on the statement of operations.

Any remaining obligations are termed **other liabilities** (long-term) and should include the non-current portion of debt and any deferred payments such as deferred taxes.

The final section of a balance sheet, **owners' equity**, should indicate the legal form of the business so the reader will know whether the business is a proprietorship, a partnership, or a corporation, and the amount of the investment made by the owner(s). The final item listed in the equity section of the balance sheet for a corporation is ordinarily the retained earnings or loss of the company from its inception.

Cash Flow Statements

Cash flow statements are prepared from the balance sheet, follow a prescribed format, and (if the balance sheet has been properly prepared) are easily produced by any of the multitude of available general ledger programs. Cash flow statements in their simplest form show cash provided by or used for operations (profits or losses), cash provided by or used for investing activities (buying or selling vehicles and other assets), and cash provided by or used for financing activities (new borrowings or repayments thereof).

While cash flow statements are very useful for banks, vendors, or potential investors (anyone who does not know the business well), in my opinion they are not particularly enlightening to management. Management usually knows the cash situation on a daily basis and has dealt with cash problems long before the formal, historical cash flow statements are prepared.

Income Statements

The income or operating statement is typically the most important of the standard financial statements to management, because a properly prepared statement is more than a historical listing of income and expense. A good statement of operations will alert management to under-performing business segments and will reflect trends that can have significant impacts on profitability in the future. Rather than simply listing costs by their generic names and subtracting the total of these costs from revenues, profitability is best managed by establishing departments to capture costs. When the departmental costs are reflected against specific revenues, profit center accounting is the result.

Computerized Accounting Systems

Many delivery companies do their invoicing by means of a separate, industry-specific dispatch, rating, billing and accounts receivable program, of which many are available. It is usually preferable in this industry, however, to use a different general ledger program to write checks, enter cash receipts, compute depreciation, make journal entries, produce canned financial statements, etc. These general ledger programs include a "standard" chart of accounts, described in the users' manual that accompanies the software package.

The standard charts of accounts that are part of the general ledger programs I have seen are not adequate for any company that has revenues greater than several hundred thousand dollars per year. These inadequate systems are typically very simple recording schemes that use two- or three-digit account numbers to provide summary revenue and expense listings, but do not provide enough detail or flexibility to create any specialized reporting for the business.

The development of a flexible chart of accounts, with the resultant financial statements and departmental structure in mind before the numbering scheme is selected, is the first step to be accomplished before the chart of accounts is input into the computer.

A Flexible Chart of Accounts

The following is the skeleton structure for the flexible chart of accounts that I installed at Mid-Counties and, with some minor modifications, at other companies. The resultant detailed chart of accounts is easy to understand and will produce the desired level of information for a delivery company when it is small, and it can be expanded to provide information adequate to manage a $100 million, multi-division company.

The basic numbering scheme and account structure is as follows:

Assets	1xxxx	
	11xxx	Current assets
	12xxx	Fixed assets
	13xxx	Other current assets
Liabilities	2xxxx	
	21xxx	Accounts payable
	22xxx	Accrued liabilities
	230xx	Payroll taxes payable
	231xx	Other taxes payable
	233xx	Other current liabilities
	29xxx	Long-term liabilities
Equity	3xxxx	
Revenue	4xxxx	
Freight Forwarding Exp	5xxxx	
Other/Misc Income	6xxxx	
Expenses	7xxxx-xxx	(the final three digits are for department #)
	710xx-xxx	Charges from payroll
	711xx-xxx	Employer portion of P/R related
	712xx-xxx	Vehicle expenses
	713xx-xxx	Depreciation
	714xx-xxx	Equipment costs
	715xx-xxx	Facilities costs
	716xx-xxx	Other costs and expenses
	717xx-xxx	Sales and Marketing expenses
	9xxxx	Taxes

Charges to the freight forwarding account (51010) can be made directly to this account or to a series of job numbers that are closed into this account. Jobs were used when we had a number of orders going on one airline flight. We used the jobs to isolate the costs for each sales invoice in order to make sure we achieved our desired profitability per shipment.

The departments we were using at Mid-Counties when the business was sold were:

Dept	Use	Revenue Acct. No.	Purpose of Revenue Acct.
105	Direct ground delivery charges (drivers and vehicles), except for First American Title	41010	Gather all ground revenue generated by Mid-Counties drivers (other than First American revenue)
106	Direct delivery charges associated with the First American Title work	41011	Capture all First American revenue generated by the dedicated First American drivers
107	Warehouse costs	41040 and 41050	Collect revenues for handling and storage
110	Operations costs		
210	Sales and marketing costs		
310	Administration costs (including interest)		
		41020	Capture revenues from freight forwarding
		41025	Capture revenue from international remail

Actual Detailed Chart of Accounts

Note that certain of the following accounts in the Equity section (3xxxx series) are required by the Peachtree general ledger program; and may not be necessary under another general ledger system.

Account ID	Account Description	Account Type
11005	Cash on Hand	Cash
11010	Cash in Bank-Comerica	Cash
11010	Cash in Bank-Coast Commercial	Cash
11030	Accounts Receivable	Accounts Receivable
11035	Allowance for Doubtful Accounts	Accounts Receivable
11037	Other Accounts receivable	Accounts Receivable
11040	Employee Advances	Other Current Assets
11050	Prepaid Rent	Other Current Assets
11051	Prepaid Insurance	Other Current Assets
11060	Prepaid Interest	Other Current Assets
11070	Prepaid Taxes	Other Current Assets
11080	Prepaid Commissions	Other Current Assets
12010	Vehicles	Fixed Assets
12015	Accumulated Deprec-Vehicles	Accumulated Deprec
12020	Furniture and Equipment	Fixed Assets
12025	Accumulated Deprec-F & E	Accumulated Deprec
12030	Leasehold Improvements	Fixed Assets
12035	Accumulated Deprec-L I	Accumulated Deprec
13010	Deposits	Other Assets
13030	Goodwill	Other Assets
13035	Less- Goodwill Amortization	Amortization
21010	Accounts Payable	Accounts Payable
21020	Accrued Payroll	Other Current Liab
21030	Interest Payable	Other Current Liab
21040	Commissions Payable	Other Current Liab
21050	Other Payables	Other Current Liab
23010	Payroll Taxes Payable	Other Current Liab
23110	Federal Income Tax Payable	Other Current Liab
23120	Franchise Tax Payable	Other Current Liab
23300	401K Deductions Payable	Other Current Liab
23301	Bonuses Payable	Other Current Liab
23302	Short-Term Notes Payable	Other Current Liab
23303	Current Portion of Long-Term Debt	Other Current Liab
23350	Deferred Revenue	Other Current Liab.
29010	Contracts Payable	Long-Term Liabilities
29020	Bank Line of Credit	Long-Term Liabilities
29030	SBA Loan	Long-Term Liabilities
29040	Bank Term Loan	Long-Term Liabilities
29110	Notes Payable-Shareholders	Long-Term Liabilities
29120	Notes Payable-Other	Long-Term Liabilities

Account ID	Account Description	Account Type
29195	Less-Current Portion Long-Term Debt	Long-Term Liabilities
31010	Capital Stock	Equity-doesn't close
32020	Current Year Net Income	Equity-gets closed
32030	Previous Retained Earnings	Equity-Retained Earnings
39004	Beginning Balance-Retained Earnings	Equity-doesn't close
39005	Retained Earnings	Equity-Retained Earnings
39999	Suspense	Expenses
41010	Deliveries by Mid-Counties Drivers	Income
41011	Deliveries by 1st American Route Drivers	Income
41015	Discounts & Allowances-MCD	Income
41020	Deliveries by Agents	Income
41025	International Remail	Income
41026	Discounts & Allowances-Agents	Income
41030	Commissions	Income
41040	Handling	Income
41050	Warehousing	Income
41060	Other	Income
42000	Shipping Charges Reimbursed	Income
45000	Gain or Loss on Vehicle Dispositions	Income
51010	Deliveries by Agents	Cost of Sales
71001-105	Salaries and Wages-Drivers	Expenses
71001-106	Salaries andWages-1stAmerican Drivers	Expenses
71001-107	Salaries and Wages-Warehouse	Expenses
71001-110	Salaries and Wages-Operations	Expenses
71001-210	Salaries and Wages-Sales	Expenses
71001-310	Salaries and Wages-Administration	Expenses
71002-105	Bonuses-Drivers	Expenses
71002-106	Bonuses-1st American Drivers	Expenses
71002-107	Bonuses-Warehouse	Expenses
71002-110	Bonuses-Operations	Expenses
71002-210	Bonuses-Sales	Expenses
71002-310	Bonuses-Administration	Expenses
71003-105	Commissions-Drivers	Expenses
71003-106	Commissions-1st American Drivers	Expenses
71003-210	Commissions-Sales	Expenses

Account ID	Account Description	Account Type
71004-105	Sick Pay-Drivers	Expenses
71004-106	Sick Pay-1st American Drivers	Expenses
71004-107	Sick Pay-Warehouse	Expenses
71004-110	Sick Pay-Operations	Expenses
71004-210	Sick Pay-Sales	Expenses
71004-310	Sick Pay-Administration	Expenses
71005-105	Vacation Pay-Drivers	Expenses
71005-106	Vacation Pay-1st American Drivers	Expenses
71005-107	Vacation Pay-Warehouse	Expenses
71005-110	Vacation Pay-Operations	Expenses
71005-210	Vacation Pay-Sales	Expenses
71005-310	Vacation Pay-Administration	Expenses
71006-105	Holiday Pay-Drivers	Expenses
71006-106	Holiday Pay-1st American Drivers	Expenses
71006-107	Holiday Pay-Warehouse	Expenses
71006-110	Holiday Pay-Operations	Expenses
71006-210	Holiday Pay-Sales	Expenses
71006-310	Holiday Pay-Administration	Expenses
71007-105	Industrial Injury-Drivers	Expenses
71007-106	Industrial Injury-1st American Drivers	Expenses
71007-107	Industrial Injury-Warehouse	Expenses
71007-110	Industrial Injury-Operations	Expenses
71008-105	Jury Duty-Drivers	Expenses
71008-106	Jury Duty-1st American Drivers	Expenses
71008-107	Jury Duty-Warehouse	Expenses
71008-110	Jury Duty-Operations	Expenses
71008-210	Jury Duty-Sales	Expenses
71008-310	Jury Duty-Administration	Expenses
71009-105	Training-Drivers	Expenses
71009-106	Training-1st American Drivers	Expenses
71009-107	Training-Warehouse	Expenses
71009-110	Training-Operations	Expenses
71009-210	Training-Sales	Expenses
71009-310	Training-Administration	Expenses
71111-105	Workers Comp Ins-Drivers	Expenses
71111-106	Workers Comp Ins-1st American	Expenses
71111-107	Workers Comp Ins-Warehouse	Expenses
71111-110	Workers Comp Ins-Operations	Expenses
71111-210	Workers Comp Ins-Sales	Expenses
71111-310	Workers Comp Ins-Administration	Expenses
71201-105	Fuel-Drivers	Expenses
71201-106	Fuel-1st American Drivers	Expenses

Account ID	Account Description	Account Type
71201-107	Fuel-Warehouse	Expenses
71201-110	Fuel-Operations	Expenses
71201-210	Fuel-Sales	Expenses
71210-310	Fuel-Administration	Expenses
71202-105	Vehicle Mileage Reimbursement	Expenses
71202-106	Vehicle Mileage Reimbursement	Expenses
71202-107	Vehicle Mileage Reimbursement	Expenses
71202-110	Vehicle Mileage Reimbursement	Expenses
71202-210	Vehicle Mileage Reimbursement	Expenses
71202-310	Vehicle Mileage Reimbursement	Expenses
71203-105	Vehicle Maintenance and Parts	Expenses
71203-106	Vehicle Maintenance and Parts	Expenses
71203-107	Vehicle Maintenance and Parts	Expenses
71203-110	Vehicle Maintenance and Parts	Expenses
71203-210	Vehicle Maintenance and Parts	Expenses
71203-310	Vehicle Maintenance and Parts	Expenses
71204-105	Vehicle Washing	Expenses
71204-106	Vehicle Washing	Expenses
71204-110	Vehicle Washing	Expenses
71204-210	Vehicle Washing	Expenses
71204-310	Vehicle Washing	Expenses
71205-105	Vehicle Registration	Expenses
71205-106	Vehicle Registration	Expenses
71205-110	Vehicle Registration	Expenses
71205-210	Vehicle Registration	Expenses
71205-310	Vehicle Registration	Expenses
71206-105	Vehicle Rental	Expenses
71206-106	Vehicle Rental	Expenses
71206-110	Vehicle Rental	Expenses
71206-210	Vehicle Rental	Expenses
71206-310	Vehicle Rental	Expenses
71207-105	Tires	Expenses
71207-106	Tires	Expenses
71207-110	Tires	Expenses
71207-210	Tires	Expenses
71207-310	Tires	Expenses
71208-106	Vehicle Allowance	Expenses
71208-105	Vehicle Allowance	Expenses
71208-110	Vehicle Allowance	Expenses
71208-210	Vehicle Allowance	Expenses
71208-310	Vehicle Allowance	Expenses
71209-105	Vehicle Physical Damage-Owned Vehicle	Expenses

Account ID	Account Description	Account Type
71209-106	Vehicle Physical Damage-Owned Vehicle	Expenses
71209-110	Vehicle Physical Damage-Owned Vehicle	Expenses
71209-210	Vehicle Physical Damage-Owned Vehicle	Expenses
71209-310	Vehicle Physical Damage-Owned Vehicle	Expenses
71210-105	Vehicle Physical Damage-Other Vehicle	Expenses
71210-106	Vehicle Physical Damage-Other Vehicle	Expenses
71212-105	Towing	Expenses
71212-106	Towing	Expenses
71213-105	Smog Permits	Expenses
71213-106	Smog Permits	Expenses
71213-110	Smog Permits	Expenses
71213-210	Smog Permits	Expenses
71213-310	Smog Permits	Expenses
71301-105	Vehicle Depreciation	Expenses
71301-106	Vehicle Depreciation	Expenses
71301-107	Vehicle Depreciation	Expenses
71301-110	Vehicle Depreciation	Expenses
71301-210	Vehicle Depreciation	Expenses
71301-310	Vehicle Depreciation	Expenses
71302-105	Furniture & Equipment Depreciation	Expenses
71302-107	Furniture & Equipment Depreciation	Expenses
71302-110	Furniture & Equipment Depreciation	Expenses
71302-210	Furniture & Equipment Depreciation	Expenses
71302-310	Furniture & Equipment Depreciation	Expenses
71303-105	Leasehold Improvements Depreciation	Expenses
71303-107	Leasehold Improvements Depreciation	Expenses
71303-110	Leasehold Improvements Depreciation	Expenses
71303-210	Leasehold Improvements Depreciation	Expenses
71303-310	Leasehold Improvements Depreciation	Expenses
71307-310	Amortization of Goodwill	Expenses
71401-105	Equipment Rentals/Leases	Expenses
71401-107	Equipment Rentals/Leases	Expenses
71401-110	Equipment Rentals/Leases	Expenses
71401-210	Equipment Rentals/Leases	Expenses
71401-310	Equipment Rentals/Leases	Expenses
71402-105	Repeaters-Radio Costs	Expenses

Account ID	Account Description	Account Type
71402-106	Repeaters-Radio Costs	Expenses
71402-110	Repeaters-Radio Costs	Expenses
71402-210	Repeaters-Radio Costs	Expenses
71402-310	Repeaters-Radio Costs	Expenses
71403-105	Pager Costs	Expenses
71403-106	Pager Costs	Expenses
71403-110	Pager Costs	Expenses
71403-210	Pager Costs	Expenses
71403-310	Pager Costs	Expenses
71404-105	Equipment Maintenance & Repair	Expenses
71404-107	Equipment Maintenance & Repair	Expenses
71404-110	Equipment Maintenance & Repair	Expenses
71404-210	Equipment Maintenance & Repair	Expenses
71404-310	Equipment Maintenance & Repair	Expenses
71405-105	Equipment Support	Expenses
71405-110	Equipment Support	Expenses
71405-210	Equipment Support	Expenses
71405-310	Equipment Support	Expenses
71406-105	Non-Capital Equipment	Expenses
71406-107	Non-Capital Equipment	Expenses
71406-110	Non-Capital Equipment	Expenses
71406-210	Non-Capital Equipment	Expenses
71406-310	Non-Capital Equipment	Expenses
71501-105	Rent	Expenses
71501-107	Rent	Expenses
71501-110	Rent	Expenses
71501-210	Rent	Expenses
71501-310	Rent	Expenses
71502-107	Janitorial	Expenses
71502-110	Janitorial	Expenses
71502-210	Janitorial	Expenses
71502-310	Janitorial	Expenses
71503-107	Utilities	Expenses
71503-110	Utilities	Expenses
71503-210	Utilities	Expenses
71503-310	Utilities	Expenses
71504-110	Water	Expenses
71504-210	Water	Expenses
71504-310	Water	Expenses
71505-107	Garbage	Expenses
71505-110	Garbage	Expenses
71506-107	Security	Expenses

Account ID	Account Description	Account Type
71506-310	Security	Expenses
71601-107	Postage	Expenses
71601-110	Postage	Expenses
71601-210	Postage	Expenses
71601-310	Postage	Expenses
71602-110	Freight-In	Expenses
71602-210	Freight-In	Expenses
71602-310	Freight-In	Expenses
71603-107	Dues & Publications	Expenses
71603-110	Dues & Publications	Expenses
71603-210	Dues & Publications	Expenses
71603-310	Dues & Publications	Expenses
71604-310	Bad Debts	Expenses
71605-105	Licenses & Fees	Expenses
71605-110	Licenses & Fees	Expenses
71605-210	Licenses & Fees	Expenses
71605-310	Licenses & Fees	Expenses
71606-105	Insurance	Expenses
71606-106	Insurance	Expenses
71606-107	Insurance	Expenses
71606-110	Insurance	Expenses
71606-210	Insurance	Expenses
71606-310	Insurance	Expenses
71607-105	Telephone	Expenses
71607-107	Telephone	Expenses
71607-110	Telephone	Expenses
71607-210	Telephone	Expenses
71607-310	Telephone	Expenses
71608-105	Travel	Expenses
71608-110	Travel	Expenses
71608-210	Travel	Expenses
71608-310	Travel	Expenses
71609-105	Seminars & Training	Expenses
71609-110	Seminars & Training	Expenses
71609-210	Seminars & Training	Expenses
71609-310	Seminars & Training	Expenses
71610-105	Recruiting	Expenses
71610-106	Recruiting	Expenses
71610-110	Recruiting	Expenses
71610-210	Recruiting	Expenses
71610-310	Recruiting	Expenses
71611-311	Legal & Accounting	Expenses

Account ID	Account Description	Account Type
71612-105	Outside Contract Services	Expenses
71612-106	Outside Contract Services	Expenses
71612-107	Outside Contract Services	Expenses
71612-110	Outside Contract Services	Expenses
71612-210	Outside Contract Services	Expenses
71612-310	Outside Contract Services	Expenses
71613-310	Bank Charges	Expenses
71614-105	Supplies	Expenses
71614-106	Supplies	Expenses
71614-107	Supplies	Expenses
71614-110	Supplies	Expenses
71614-210	Supplies	Expenses
71614-310	Supplies	Expenses
71615-105	Forms	Expenses
71615-106	Forms	Expenses
71615-107	Forms	Expenses
71615-110	Forms	Expenses
71615-210	Forms	Expenses
71615-310	Forms	Expenses
71616-310	Interest	Expenses
71617-110	DMV Operating Authority	Expenses
71618-105	Bridge Tolls	Expenses
71619-105	Parking	Expenses
71619-106	Parking	Expenses
71619-110	Parking	Expenses
71619-210	Parking	Expenses
71619-310	Parking	Expenses
71620-105	Maps	Expenses
71620-106	Maps	Expenses
71620-110	Maps	Expenses
71621-105	Gifts	Expenses
71621-106	Gifts	Expenses
71621-107	Gifts	Expenses
71621-110	Gifts	Expenses
71621-210	Gifts	Expenses
71621-310	Gifts	Expenses
71622-105	Dry Ice	Expenses
71623-105	Freight Damage	Expenses
71623-107	Freight Damage	Expenses
71623-210	Freight Damage	Expenses
71624-310	Payroll Preparation	Expenses
71625-110	Answering Service	Expenses
71626-105	Office Food, Drinks, Etc.	Expenses

Account ID	Account Description	Account Type
71626-106	Office Food, Drinks, Etc	Expenses
71626-107	Office Food, Drinks, Etc.	Expenses
71626-110	Office Food, Drinks, Etc.	Expenses
71626-210	Office Food, Drinks, Etc	Expenses
71626-310	Office Food, Drinks, Etc.	Expenses
71627-110	Memberships	Expenses
71627-310	Memberships	Expenses
71628-210	Charitable Contributions	Expenses
71628-310	Charitable Contributions	Expenses
71629-105	Industrial Injuries	Expenses
71629-106	Industrial Injuries	Expenses
71629-107	Industrial Injuries	Expenses
71630-110	C.O.D. Amounts	Expenses
71631-105	Property Taxes	Expenses
71631-110	Property Taxes	Expenses
71631-210	Property Taxes	Expenses
71631-310	Property Taxes	Expenses
71632-105	Uniforms	Expenses
71632-106	Uniforms	Expenses
71632-110	Uniforms	Expensee
71633-105	Retirement	Expenses
71633-106	Retirement	Expenses
71633-107	Retirement	Expenses
71633-110	Retirement	Expenses
71633-210	Retirement	Expenses
71633-310	Retirement	Expenses
71634-110	Non-Revenue Shipping	Expenses
71634-210	Non-Revenue Shipping	Expenses
71634-310	Non-Revenue Shipping	Expenses
71675-105	Miscellaneous	Expenses
71675-110	Miscellaneous	Expenses
71675-210	Miscellaneous	Expenses
71675-310	Miscellaneous	Expenses
71701-110	Advertising	Expenses
71701-210	Advertising	Expenses
71701-310	Advertising	Expenses
71702-210	Literature	Expenses
71702-310	Literature	Expenses
71703-210	Brochures	Expenses
71703-310	Brochures	Expenses
71704-310	Entertainment	Expenses
71705-110	Funds Advanced	Expenses

Account ID	Account Description	Account Type
71706-210	Sales Commissions	Expenses
71707-105	Meetings	Expenses
71707-106	Meetings	Expenses
71707-107	Meetings	Expenses
71707-110	Meetings	Expenses
71707-210	Meetings	Expenses
71707-310	Meetings	Expenses
70708-210	Prospect Lists	Expenses
91010	Franchise Tax	Expenses
91020	Federal Income Tax	Expenses

Various Income Statement Formats

Following is operating information in several different formats. The information was produced by using the above chart of accounts.

Below is an income statement in the simplest format provided by the popular small business general ledger programs. We did not use this format at Mid-Counties.

Current Month

Revenues		$256,718.95
Expenses		
	Deliveries by Agents	$114,131.43
	Salaries and Wages	47,613.42
	Bonuses	1,303.19
	Vacation Pay	150.16
	Workers Comp Insurance	2,110.00
	Fuel	4,919.87
	Mileage Reimbursement	2,994.52
	Vehicle Maintenance and Parts	2,165.19
	Vehicle Washing	302.50
	Vehicle Registration	1,706.00
	Tires	874.44
	Vehicle Allowance	1,159.54
	Depreciation	6,236.85
	Amortization	53.53
	Equipment Rentals/Leases	368.47
	Repeaters-Radio Costs	1,467.10
	Pager Costs	29.86
	Equipment Maintenance & Repair	622 .11
	Equipment Support	448.00
	Rent	6,700.00
	Janitorial	200.00

Utilities	869.47
Postage	10.00
Dues & Publications	140.00
Bad Debt Expense	122.64
Insurance	9,093.18
Telephone	954.87
Legal & Accounting	595.00
Outside Contract Services	610.00
Bank Charges	457.25
Supplies	582.74
Interest	5,519.33
Bridge Tolls	24.90
Parking	1.00
Gifts	53.88
Payroll Preparation	428.30
Answering Service	130.05
Office Food, Drinks, Etc.	66.20
Memberships	187.50
Advertising	2,058.66
Sales Commissions	20,550.00
Meetings	198.79

Total Expenses	238,209.94
Income Before Taxes	$18,509.01

Using the same chart of accounts, the following format provides more useful information. At Mid-Counties we used this format for tax preparation only.

Current Month

Revenues:

Deliveries by Agents	$187,601.35	
Deliveries by Mid-Counties	64,119.82	
Storage & Handling	4,997.78	
Total Revenues	$256,718.95	100%

Expenses:

Deliveries by Agents		114,131.43 44%
Salaries & Wages	47,613.42	
Bonuses	1,303.19	
Vacation Pay	150.16	
Payroll Costs		49,066.77 19%
Workers Comp Costs		2,110.00 1%
Fuel	4,919.87	
Vehicle Mileage Reimbursement	2,994.52	
Vehicle Maintenance and Parts	2,165.19	
Vehicle Washing	302.50	
Vehicle Registration	1,706.00	
Tires	874.44	

Vehicle Allowance	1,159.54		
Vehicle Expenses		14,122.06	6%
Depreciation	6,236.85		
Amortization	53.53		
Depreciation & Amortization		6,290.38	2%
Equipment Rentals/Leases	368.47		
Repeater-Radio Costs	1,467.10		
Pager Costs	29.86		
Equipment Maintenance & Repair	622.11		
Equipment Support	448.00		
Equipment Costs		2,935.54	1%
Rent	6,700.00		
Janitorial	200.00		
Utilities	869.47		
Facilities Costs		7,769.47	3%
Postage	10.00		
Dues and Publications	140.00		
Bad Debt Expense	122.64		
Insurance	9,093.18		
Telephone	954.87		
Legal & Accounting	595.00		
Outside Contract Services	610.00		
Bank Charges	457.25		
Supplies	582.74		
Interest	5,519.33		
Bridge Tolls	24.90		
Parking	1.00		
Gifts	53.88		
Payroll Processing	428.30		
Answering Service	130.05		
Office Food, Drinks, Etc.	66.20		
Memberships	187.50		
Other Costs & Expenses		18,976.84	8%
Advertising	2,058.66		
Commissions	20,550.00		
Meetings	198.79		
Sales & Marketing		22,807.45	9%
Total Expenses		238,209.94	93%
Income Before Taxes		$18,509.01	7%

Using the same chart of accounts, the following format presents the information in a manner that allows the user to understand the business's areas of operation. This was the primary income statement format that we distributed to outsiders; with the balance sheet and statement of cash flows, it made up the financial package for banks, Dun & Bradstreet, etc.

This format closely resembles the income statement format used by most large or public corporations.

Income Statement
Month of XXXXX

Revenues	Current Month	%	Year To Date	%
Deliveries by				
Mid-Counties Drivers	$44,042.77	17	$124,651.47	23
Deliveries by First				
American Drivers	20,077.05	8	58,496.80	11
Deliveries by Agents	22,632.62	9	96,157.16	18
International Remail	164,968.73	64	248,005.09	45
Storage & Handling	4,997.78	2	16,017.35	3
Total Revenues	256,718.95	100	543,327,87	100
Cost of revenues				
Deliveries by				
Mid-Counties Drivers a	35,667.22	14	97,713.32	18
Deliveries by First				
American Drivers b	13,701.64	5	38,068.70	7
Delivery by Agents c	114,131.43	44	214,575.16	39
Storage & Handling d	8,567.29	4	25,123.64	4
Operations e	15,488.33	6	45,455.27	8
Total Cost of Revenues	187,555.91	73	420,936.09	77
Gross margin	69,163.04	27	122,391.78	23
Expenses				
Sales f	33,048.53	13	61,290.26	11
Administration g	12,086.17	5	32,738.90	6
Interest h	5,519.33	2	21,236.34	4
Total expenses	50,654.03	20	115,265.50	21
Other				
Gain (loss) on sale-assets	0		5,200.00	1
Income (loss) before taxes	$18,509.01	7	$12,326.28	2

a – Department 105
b – Department 106
c – Account 51010
d – Department 107
e – Department 110

f – Department 210
g – Department 310 less interest expense which is shown separately as h
h – Separate line item from Department 310

Examples of Departmental Reporting

The six departmental expense summaries follow. They are part of the monthly financial package that, together with the above income statement, the balance sheet and the statement of cash flows, made up the package that was distributed to management. Our general ledger program allowed us to compare the actual figures to budgeted amounts or to last year's figures.

Month of xxxx
Departmental Expense Summary
Deliveries by Mid-Counties Drivers
Department 105

	Current Month	Year To Date
Expenses		
Salaries and Wages-Drivers	$12,676.26	$37,213.75
Bonuses-Drivers	549.75	549.75
Vacation Pay	150.16	274.61
Workers Comp Insurance	1,900.00	5,700.00
Fuel	4,563.34	10,882.20
Vehicle Maintenance and Parts	2,165.19	4,964.49
Vehicle Washing	120.00	120.00
Vehicle Registration	1,706.00	2,831.00
Tires	874.44	1,095.95
Towing	0.00	682.50
Vehicle Depreciation	3,923.70	11,771.10
Furniture & Equipment Depreciation	5.00	15.00
Repeaters-Radio Costs	426.33	1,255.27
Pager Costs	0.00	64.14
Non-Capital Equipment	0.00	5.83
Rent	750.00	1,910.00
Licenses & Fees	0.00	15.00
Insurance	5,767.27	17,356.28
Recruiting	0.00	76.77
Bridge Tolls	24.90	36.90
Parking	1.00	4.25
Gifts	53.88	53.88
Office Food, Drinks, Etc	10.00	46.18
Industrial Injuries	0.00	788.47
Total Expenses	$35,667.22	$97,713.32

Month of xxxx
Departmental Expense Summary
Deliveries by 1st American Route Drivers
Department 106

	Current Month	Year To Date
Expenses		
Salaries and Wages-		
1st American Route Drivers	$10,261.69	$27,905.09
Workers Comp Insurance	55.00	165.00
Vehicle Mileage Reimbursement	2,994.52	9,103.17
Pager Costs	29.86	224.55
Insurance	360.57	670.89
Total Expenses	$13,701.64	$38,068.70

Month of xxxx
Departmental Expense Summary
Storage & Handling
Department 107

	Current Month	Year To Date
Expenses		
Salaries and Wages-Warehouse	$4,569.46	$13,750.34
Bonuses-Warehouse	0.00	164.92
Vacation Pay	0.00	187.77
Workers Comp Insurance	50.00	150.00
Fuel	15.03	15.03
Furniture & Equipment Depreciation	83.85	251.55
Leasehold Improvements Depreciation	99.67	299.01
Equipment Rentals/Leases	101.50	101.50
Rent	1,900.00	4,950.00
Janitorial	50.00	150.00
Utilities	205.33	432.69
Security	0.00	154.50
Postage	10.00	351.00
Insurance	972.26	2,327.46
Supplies	482.09	1,755.47
Office Food, Drinks, Etc	28.10	82.40
Total Expenses	$8,567.29	$25,123.64

Month of xxxx
Departmental Expense Summary
Operations
Department 110

	Current Month	Year To Date
Expenses		
Salaries and Wages-Operations	$9,521.85	$26,995.39
Vacation Pay	0.00	310.18
Workers Comp Insurance	45.00	135.00
Furniture & Equipment Depreciation	1,166.62	3,423.22
Equipment Rentals/Leases	157.97	631.76
Repeaters-Radio Costs	428.41	1,140.42
Equipment Maintenance & Repair	272.16	497.51
Equipment Support	448.00	2,223.00
Rent	1,900.00	4,950.00
Janitorial	50.00	150.00
Utilities	253.48	530.93
Garbage	0.00	6.00
Postage	0.00	333.00
Freight In	0.00	17.81
Dues & Publications	15.00	15.00
Licenses & Fees	0.00	44.96
Insurance	375.98	1,096.78
Telephone	345.06	1,046.43
Outside Contract Services	250.00	500.00
Supplies	100.65	361.15
DMV Operating Authority	0.00	475.00
Answering Service	130.05	375.85
Office Food, Drinks, Etc	28.10	186.77
Non-Revenue Shipping	0.00	9.11
Total Expenses	$15,488.33	$45,455.27

Month of xxxx
Departmental Expense Summary
Sales & Marketing
Department 210

	Current Month	Year To Date
Expenses		
Salaries and Wages-Sales	$5,518.40	$16,931.12
Bonuses	753.44	1,536.27
Workers Comp Insurance	35.00	105.00
Fuel	341.50	561.15
Vehicle Washing	67.85	67.85
Vehicle Depreciation	500.32	1500.96
Furniture & Equipment Depreciation	12.94	38.82
Repeaters-Radio Costs	566.22	953.42
Rent	1,075.00	2,945.00
Janitorial	50.00	150.00
Utilities	205.33	432.68
Dues & Publications	0.00	322.17
Insurance	749.00	2,247.00
Telephone	404.88	1,108.58
Advertising	2,058.66	6,269.28
Sales Commissions	20,550.00	25,809.95
Meetings	159.99	311.01
Total Expenses	$33,048.53	$61,290.26

Month of xxxx
Departmental Expense Summary
Administration
Department 310

	Current Month	Year To Date
Expenses		
Salaries and Wages-Operations	$5,065.76	$15,332.65
Workers Comp Insurance	25.00	75.00
Fuel	0.00	129.53
Vehicle Maintenance and Parts	0.00	633.02
Vehicle Washing	114.65	114.65
Vehicle Allowance	1,159.54	3,478.62
Furniture & Equipment Depreciation	444.75	1,334.25
Amortization of Goodwill	53.53	160.59
Equipment Rentals/Leases	109.00	264.70
Repeaters-Radio Costs	46.14	136.12
Equipment Maintenance & Repair	349.95	349.95
Rent	1,075.00	2,945.00
Janitorial	50.00	150.00
Utilities	205.33	432.67
Postage	0.00	334.00
Dues & Publications	125.00	145.00
Bad Debt Expense	122.64	<1,530.95>
Licenses & Fees	0.00	20.00
Insurance	868.10	2,614.50
Telephone	204.93	320.10
Legal & Accounting	595.00	1,327.00
Outside Contract Services	360.00	1,375.00
Bank Charges	457.25	871.75
Supplies	0.00	80.00
Interest*	5,519.33	21,236.34
Payroll Preparation	428.30	987.15
Office Food, Drinks, Etc	0.00	82.30
Memberships	187.50	537.50
Meetings	38.80	38.80
Total Expenses	$17,605.50	$53,975.24

*For financial statement preparation, Interest is removed from this department's
totals and shown as a separate line item.

It can be cumbersome working with this level of detail, but when
the information is printed by department, the data becomes more
manageable. When several months are compared or when budget

information has been entered to this level, it becomes easy to pinpoint spending problems.

Income Statement by Profit Center

We also produced the following top-level, confidential income statement. It was distributed to the profit center managers because it showed gross margin by profit center; it was used to determine salary levels and bonuses for these managers.

Month of xxxx
Income Statement by Profit Center

	Deliveries by Mid-Counties	Deliveries by Agents	Storage & Handling	Total
Revenue	$64,119.82	$187,601.35	$4,997.78	$256,718.95
Reclassification i		3,569.51	<3,569.51>	
Direct Costs	49,368.86 a	114,131.43 b	8,567.29 c	172,067.58
Indirect Costs d	3,868.47	11,619.86		15,488.33
Total	53,237.33	129,320.80	4,997.78	187,555.91
Gross Margin	10,882.49	58,280.55	0.00	69,163.04
	17 %	31 %		27 %

Expenses h	
Sales & Marketing	33,048.53 e
Administration	12,086.17 f
Interest	5,519.33 g
Total	50,654.03
	20 %
Income (Loss) Before Taxes	$18,509.01
	7 %

This profit center report can be run for year-to-date numbers also, if desired.

a — Drivers departments (2)
b — Invoices from agents
c — Warehouse department
d — Operations department
e — Sales department
f — Administration, less interest, which is shown in g
g — Separate line item
h — The expense departments can be spread among the profit centers based on sales or some other allocation method if top management

believes that is more meaningful than showing them in total as I have done.

i —   This loss is transferred to the Deliveries by Agents profit center (freight forwarding), because the same manager managed our freight forwarding and warehouse operations and had the pricing authority to affect the revenues (i.e., gross margins) within and between these two cost centers.

Since our pricing schemes were set up to produce 30 percent margins for our profit centers, the Income Statement by Profit Center showed that something was amiss in the Deliveries by Mid-Counties profit center. We had to study the departmental expense reports for departments 105 and 106 to see if spending was out of line. This review indicated that our driver wages were too high in department 105. (This was because the economy was slowing down and our on-demand business was drying up.) We had to reduce the size of the on-demand driver group.

This type of reporting package, with clear departmental cost breakdowns for all expenses—*based on a good chart of accounts*—together with any of the popular general ledger programs, will provide management with quick answers to profit problems or questions without the necessity for a large finance staff.

Key Balance Sheet Ratios and Operating Data | 4

Subjects covered in this chapter
- *Balance sheet format*
- *Key ratios that reflect financial strength*
- *Key ratios that portend profitability*
- *Managing by the numbers*

A well run company develops a finite number of key ratios and operating data that quickly give the reader a snapshot of the company's well being. Any key ratios computed from the balance sheet can be compared to standards or norms for all companies. However, ratios or data that are produced from the income statement tend to be industry-specific and are generally not comparable to ratios or data for companies outside the industry.

As I indicated in the previous chapter, balance sheets are generally used to determine credit worthiness, and so ratios produced from balance sheets indicate relative financial strength when compared to standard ratios for all companies.

In the previous chapter we examined income statements in several formats designed to enhance profitability and control. In this chapter the balance sheet is reviewed from the standpoint of ratios that indicate financial strength, plus other measurements that can portend profitability issues.

Balance Sheet
at xxxx
ASSETS

Current Assets		
Cash on Hand	$25.00	
Cash in Bank	18,007.21	
Accounts Receivable	205,316.90	
Prepaid Insurance	11,294.10	
Total Current Assets		$234,643.21
Property and Equipment		
Vehicles	349,515.60	
Accumulated Depr-Vehicles	<227,714.85>	
Furniture and Equipment	113,645.43	
Accumulated Depr- Furn & Equip	<65,554.00>	
Leasehold Improvements	5,980.00	
Accumulated Depr-Leasehold Imp	<2,099.91>	
Net Property and Equipment		173,772.27
Other Assets		
Deposits	457.98	
Prepaid Rent	9,500.00	
Goodwill	26,977.00	
Less-Amortization	<7,379.59>	
Total Other Assets		29,555.39
Total Assets		$437,970.87

LIABILITIES and CAPITAL

Current Liabilities		
Accrued Payroll	$18,044.97	
Payroll Taxes Payable	6,607.64	
Accounts Payable	126,954.72	
Current portion of Long term Debt	45,000.00	
Total Current Liabilities		$196,607.33
Long-Term Liabilities		
Contracts Payable	52,196.27	
Bank Line of Credit	105,000.00	
Notes Payable-Shareholders	61,857.25	
Less-Current Portion LTD	<45,000.00>	
Total Long-Term Liabilities		174,053.52
Equity		
Capital Stock	20,000.00	
Retained Earnings	34,983.74	
Net Income	12,326.28	
Total Equity		67,310.02
Total Liabilities and Equity		$437,970.87

Metrology that Indicates Ability to Pay Debt

Metrology

The relationship between current assets and current liabilities is significant: it determines the working capital of the company. Current assets less current liabilities produces the working capital. Current assets divided by current liabilities produces the current ratio. Bankers or other lenders look for a current ratio for any company of 2:1. With this current ratio, a company has twice as many assets that are cash or close to being cash as current bills, and it should have no problem paying its normal liabilities.

The working capital and current ratio for the above balance sheet are shown below:

Current Assets	$234,643.21
Current Liabilities	196,607.33
Working Capital	$ 38,035.88
Current Ratio	1.1:1

While this current ratio is too low, there are several mitigating factors. Since Mid-Counties had been burned a few times with large accounts receivable write-offs, I had accumulated a $25,000 reserve for bad debts; that was netted against the accounts receivable balance included in the above current assets. Also, the company had several large customers that paid their bills within 10 days of receiving them, and since Mid-Counties invoiced every week, a significant percentage of the current month's billings had already been paid by the financial statement date.

As a company gets larger and management becomes further removed from day-to-day financial details, many companies show a different ratio, called the **quick ratio**, in their weekly management meetings. In the transportation industry, because there are no inventories of product for sale, the current ratio and quick ratio are generally similar. The quick ratio is the sum of cash, receivables and marketable securities to current liabilities. Some companies, in an attempt to measure instant bill paying ability, do not show total receivables in their quick ratio. They include only receivables expected to be collected over the next 30 days. This indicates to management whether or not the company will be able to pay all its current liabilities within 30 days.

All accounts receivable (A/R) programs now produce aged receivable lists, from which companies do their A/R collection work. Receivables over 90 days old are a real problem for any company, since lenders will not allow them as security for loans. They also require an enormous amount of collection work. So, the amount of old receivables, or their percentage of total receivables, is another item that is generally reported weekly to management.

Another item that management should track to stay on top of bill paying ability is the **number of days' sales in accounts receivable.** I have always computed this number by simply adding each day's sales on account backwards from the date of the accounts receivable balance until the daily sales equaled the total receivables. I then counted the number of days it took to reach this amount. For a company (like some freight forwarders) that does not bill its customers until it receives invoices from its vendors (which must be marked up to get the amount invoiced), the actual date of the invoice is not especially meaningful, because the company tends to do invoicing only on certain days of the week. These companies must take their sales for two or three months and divide that total by 60 or 90 to get their average days' sales. This number should be divided into the accounts receivable balance to determine the number of days' sales in accounts receivable. An example of a calculation of days' sales in A/R is as follows—Gross A/R divided by the average days' sales = Days' sales in A/R, where the average days' sales are determined by dividing the sum of the last two month's sales registers by the number of days in the two months.

One final ratio that is important to lenders is the **ratio of total debt to equity.** The number they look for in this ratio is 1:1 or less. The debt-to-equity ratio is considered an indication of the company's ability to withstand adverse conditions, such as a prolonged recession or even an act such as the September 11 attack. The debt-to-equity ratio for the above balance sheet is as follows:

Total Liabilities	$370,660.85
Total Equity	67,310.02
Ratio of Debt to Equity	5.5:1

A high debt to equity ratio like the above number is a real problem for banks and other lenders that depend on the long-term viability of the company for repayment. On the other hand, this situation is common in small companies owned by one or only a few persons who take most of the profits of the company for their compensation. This practice does not provide for the accumulation of a large retained earnings balance, and therefore, the equity section of the balance sheet does not increase as the company grows. In such cases, the lender will usually consider the net worth of the owner(s) in addition to the financial strength of the company before granting a loan.

In addition to the key ratios described above, another interesting calculation for delivery companies that own their own vehicles (an asset-based company) is to divide the net book value of their vehicle fleet plus equipment that supports it by the revenue produced by the vehicles (annually). This calculation shows how much **investment is required to produce a dollar in revenue**. This information cannot be obtained from the above financial statements because they are not shown as of the end of the year, although at Mid-Counties we found that it required an investment of somewhere around $.33 to produce $1.00 in revenue. Some industries need an investment of $1.00 or more to generate $1.00 in sales. I have read that a McDonald's building and equipment cost a minimum of $2.5 million and the average revenue per restaurant is around $1.7 million. This turns out to be an investment of $1.47 to produce $1.00 in sales.

Of course, if a delivery service uses independent contractors that provide their own vehicles, the business would not be considered an asset based company, and would eliminate the necessity of making the large investment to buy vehicles in order to generate revenues.

A final calculation that should be made monthly is to divide the year-to-date earnings by the net worth of the company and convert this number to an annual percentage, so the owners can determine if their investment in the company is producing returns similar to or better than they could earn from a different investment (**return on investment**). This calculation is usually not made if the company is wholly owned by its president, because this calculation does not take into consideration the salary and other benefits received by the president.

Key Data Affecting Profitability

Since for a delivery company, most profits are generated by the drivers, management should see a report, preferably every day but at least every week, that shows the hourly revenue of every driver on the payroll that day or that week, plus the average revenue for all drivers for the period. These numbers should be compared to the company's expected (standard) revenue per hour.

Drivers are often required to work overtime, so management needs to see detailed payroll costs (wages plus benefits) for each driver on the same basis as the revenue report above. These numbers should be compared to the company's expected driver cost per hour.

The multiple of each driver's payroll cost to the revenue produced should be shown, and the average multiple for all drivers in total for the period should be shown. The revenue produced by each driver should be at least three times his payroll costs plus benefits.

The number of deliveries per driver is another factor that should be reported. This information should also be reported by the hour for each driver, in total for all drivers each day, and for the management meeting, by the average for all drivers for the week. If management sees drivers making an average of three or four on-demand deliveries per hour and yet their revenue per hour is under target, this generally indicates that prices are too low.

The miles driven per day and per week should be shown for each driver. Revenue per mile driven is another important number that should be available daily and the average reported at the weekly management meeting.

These statistics are critical in managing the profitability of the company. The details by driver will show which drivers are not producing to expectations, and the overall averages will give an assessment of profitability of the company on a daily and weekly basis.

On-going, long-term profitability is the first step in producing balance sheets that reflect the appropriate ratios that lenders and vendors look for before granting credit to a company. However, these ratios do not result automatically. Management must be vigilant in collecting and managing these metrics to make sure they tell the proper story.

Reporting Key Ratios and Data

Top management should receive the following key information weekly, for review and consideration at a management meeting which should be held a day or two after the end of each week. Operations management should receive most of this information daily.

- Revenue generated by each driver for each day and by the hour, with totals for the week.

- Payroll costs, increased by a percentage for benefits, by each driver for each day, with totals for the week.

- Daily revenue generated by each driver divided by payroll costs plus benefits for each day, also calculated for the week (drivers that produce markup of less than three are not contributing to the planned profitability of the company).

- Number of deliveries made each day and each hour worked for each driver, plus average houly deliveries for all drivers for week.

- Number of miles driven each day for every driver.

- Weekly revenue per mile for each driver and on average for all drivers for the week.

A company's books should be closed promptly when the accrued payroll numbers are known for the month (usually not longer than three weeks after the end of the month), and the following key financial information should be presented at the first management meeting after the books are closed and the monthly financial statements are prepared.

- Amount of working capital
  Shows funds available for paying available bills.

- Current ratio
  Shows overall debt paying ability.

- Quick ratio
  Shows ability to pay bills on hand.

- Return on equity
  Shows percentage return on investment. Theoretically, should be more than owners could get on another investment (i.e., savings account, bonds, etc.).

- Days' sales in accounts receivable
  Identifies potential cash problems.

- Accounts receivable aging
  Identifies potential cash problems.

Pricing |5|

Subjects covered in this chapter
- *Comparison of pricing by overnight services, truckers and couriers*
- *Courier on-demand rates per mile*
- *Pricing additional transportation services*

Pricing is probably the most important and difficult discipline involved in managing a successful delivery company, though it usually receives much less attention than sales, operations or cost control. Many businesses are so afraid they will lose customers that they maintain the same prices for years at a time with absolutely no changes.

When starting a delivery business, many owners just copy the rates of an established company that operates within their service area, or even undercut these rates. The owner of a new business uses this method of pricing because he believes he needs to provide a potential customer with a reason to use a new service. However, this method of pricing is inappropriate over the long run. When a company's rates are too low, its long-term existence is in jeopardy, and even if the company is able to stay afloat with marginal rates, life for management becomes miserable because of the constant need for funds to pay current bills. An owner must remember that, in addition to covering the costs to provide the delivery, rates must also provide enough margin to cover all selling and administrative costs and still provide adequate profits for growth. Customers are accustomed to annual rate increases from FedEx, DHL and UPS, so they are not surprised when they receive notice of an increase from their other carriers. If rates are increased every year, there is ordinarily no reason to impose a large rate increase (10 percent or more) on customers. Customers are always more willing to accept an increase in the range of 2 to 5 percent than they are a larger one, even if rates had been unchanged for years.

In general, pricing for delivery companies should be based on miles driven, time spent, and costs associated with the size of the vehicle required. With this in mind, a delivery company needs to generate a minimum of between $35.00 and $50.00 per hour from its drivers, depending on its cost structure and the delivery services it offers. Its customers, on the other hand, want to have some sort of a predetermined rate so they can decide whether or not to use a particular service. For this reason, most delivery companies publish rates for specific types of deliveries and then add additional services that can increase the base rates when appropriate.

Contrast this method of pricing with the way an auto mechanic charges for repairing a vehicle. Historically, they charged $60.00 - $75.00 per hour plus parts, and they used to break out the exact time spent on each sub-job. They have increased their pricing over the years to a flat rate per job as vehicles have become more computerized and electronic. It is now not unusual to get a $1,000 bill from your mechanic for four hours' work that includes only a few dollars for parts, and they have stopped showing a labor charge per hour. They have no compunction about charging an owner $250.00 an hour for their labor. A delivery service must have the same mentality when establishing its rates, so that when orders fit together, its drivers can bring in similarly high revenues per hour.

Local Truckers

Truckers have developed a simple pricing scheme based on weight with a low minimum charge that encourages multiple deliveries of heavy items. The minimum charge is often not even spelled out on their rate sheets. For example, if their rates begin at $.08 per lb, they might show that $.08 deliveries start at 202 lb and continue through 1000 lb. Therefore, their minimum charge would be $16.16. Of course, they do not want to generate many $16.16 invoices because they cannot make money delivering small packages in a tractor-trailer. Trucker rates decrease as weight increases, although their published tariffs usually do not go below

$.04 per lb. They can, of course, drop their prices for contracted, scheduled large loads and sometimes will go as low as $.02 per lb. It all boils down to how much they can make per hour. A good truck route can bring in $1,000 or more on most days.

Trucking companies that serve larger areas (interstate) often have a similar pricing scheme, but like the national overnight companies, they usually incorporate zones and often have different rates for different commodities.

Truckers that specialize in single, longer-range deliveries (hot shots) are more like on-demand couriers, but they usually do not have rate sheets because each delivery is unique.

The National Overnight Services

Since every delivery company is to some extent in competition with FedEx, UPS and other overnight package services, certain aspects of those services' operations as well as their pricing schemes must be taken into consideration when the company sets its prices or establishes services. The competition with the overnight package services relates to their overnight and slower business. Their same day delivery prices are higher than courier prices.

No delivery service can successfully compete on price with UPS for small package ground deliveries within one of their zones. However, while those UPS deliveries may be made the following day, they are not guaranteed for overnight delivery, and this has opened up the local and even national overnight business to other carriers.

If a local delivery service wants to compete with the national package companies, they must understand some of their operating procedures.

Pickup cutoff times
While the national companies continue to extend their cutoff times for pickups, they do not work late in the evening, which has provided a market for evening pickups by local delivery services. Of course, the local service must deliver these goods, and the

issue becomes how to price this work. Are they to be priced as same day or next day deliveries? Some companies, such as California Overnight, were formed to serve the late pickup niche and have grown very large with their emphasis on evening work. Most customers will want the company making the pickup to arrange shipment and delivery when the package must go out of the area. This has put many local delivery services into the freight forwarder business.

Package size and weight

Over the last few years, the national overnight firms have expanded their capabilities to include handling freight of all sizes and weights, by ground as well as air. Because of the convenience of dealing with the overnight companies, they have taken a chunk of the business that previously went to truckers and freight forwarders. However, the national overnight companies, with their massive overhead for order taking, tracking and billing, are not as price-effective as companies with fewer employees, such as freight forwarders and local or regional truckers. This, then, has provided a niche for low-priced companies that typically provide a more limited range of services. In general, the national overnight companies tend to compete more on the basis of faster, better service, and not on the basis of lowest price, except in the case of letters and other very low-weight envelopes and packages.

Delivery times

Over the last few years, the national overnight companies have improved their delivery times (earlier in the day), just as they have extended the times available for pickups. These early delivery times make it hard to compete on the basis of more timely deliveries; however, because of the millions of packages the overnight companies handle every day, they are more prone to make delivery errors.

At Mid-Counties, we generated a significant portion of our local delivery revenue from DHL, Airborne, RPS and FedEx. A major portion of this business was, for us, same day deliveries of packages that could not be delivered by the drivers of the overnight companies. Much of this business resulted from bad addresses, wrong zip codes, no zip codes, packages addressed to post office box numbers, and sorting errors made by the overnight companies.

Mid-Counties was never able to do any work for UPS, and we knew of no local companies that did. However, UPS-Ground was well known for its delivery errors, and we had a number of customers that distrusted UPS so much that they would go out of their way to use us when they had particularly important packages to be delivered.

Pricing policies
The national overnight companies all charge by the package and ordinarily assign a separate bill of lading number to each one. This results in many multiple-package deliveries that are one or more packages short, a source of great irritation to the customers. Because of this problem, a real business opportunity for the independent delivery company is to price its delivery not by the package, but by the stop. At Mid-Counties, we priced all our deliveries by the stop and included a competitive weight charge. We followed this pricing strategy for our same day deliveries, our next day and deferred deliveries, and our domestic and international air shipments. We found that with this pricing strategy, we became competitive even with the UPS local ground charges when the order included as few as six packages and each package weighed over five pounds. And our rates were for guaranteed next day delivery, while the UPS deliveries were not. (See the Mid-Counties Delivery Service rate sheet beginning on page 62 for our overnight pricing details.)

Couriers

On-demand deliveries
Couriers ordinarily specialize in same day deliveries, on-demand and routed. For their on-demand work, they typically offer at least four same day delivery options: The first is direct—where the first available driver is dispatched to the pickup and then routed directly to the delivery location with no stops. The others are 1-2 hour, 2-4 hour, and 5 hour deliveries. These deliveries are ordinarily priced by the mile, and since there is more opportunity

to combine deliveries with each slower option, the base rate decreases as the time available for delivery increases. The underlying concept is to produce sustainable gross margins of at least 35 percent from on-demand activities.

In my business, I found that the area we covered was so large that sometimes it was impossible to make deliveries within a 5 hour time period, so we increased the number of on-demand options (to five) to provide us with more time. And our options as described in our rate sheet were worded specifically to provide us with even more time to make our deliveries. When we missed a deadline because the weather was bad or our driver was tied up in traffic, etc., this pricing scheme allowed us to charge the customer at a lower rate for a slower delivery. (See the Mid-Counties rate sheet at 63).

The rates per mile and minimum charges for the fastest same day options must be high, because of the nature of the business (no chance for consolidations). Our rate per mile for direct deliveries was $2.75, with a minimum charge of $48.00. The minimum charge was very important because we had several high tech companies that used us to pick up from a number of their suppliers less than five miles from their manufacturing facilities. To these companies, cost was never a concern. They wanted those parts as fast as they could get them. Most of these deliveries took less than 30 minutes from dispatch to delivery, and sometimes we would get four or five calls a day for direct deliveries from each customer. The minimum charges helped make this segment of our same day business nicely profitable.

On the other hand, when we could not release a driver for a direct delivery, we told the customer we would do it on a two hour (next fastest). They sometimes grumbled, but almost always would go along with our best efforts.

Our most popular same day delivery was always our two hour delivery, which we priced at $2.20 per mile with a $32.00 minimum. This service was popular because it took roughly an hour to get from our office in Santa Cruz to San Jose and vice versa. It was by far the most common route we ran every day, and most of our customers realized that if they wanted something transported between these locations, a direct delivery was not much faster than a two hour. However, if this run, from pickup to delivery, was 40 miles, our two hour charge was $88.00 (or $44.00 per hour if there was no weight involved and the driver returned empty). This compared to $110.00 for a direct delivery; however, if a courier company can average $44.00 per hour for all of its drivers, it should be nicely profitable.

Our other on-demand deliveries were our four hour at $1.65 per mile, our six hour at $1.38 per mile, and our slowest same day delivery, our eight hour at $1.10 per hour. As mentioned above, the four and six hour options were really for Mid-Counties' convenience and few customers actually requested them. They were default rates called for by the time of day an order was placed with our customer service. (See the restrictions on times when an order must be called-in as shown in the " Same Day Service Availability" table in the rate sheet at page 64.) Besides the restrictions by when an order must be received, if we missed a two hour delivery for some reason, we used the four or six hour rate, depending when the delivery was made. Without these rates, we would have had to drop all the way to our eight hour rate.

Note from our rate sheet that the customer was required to call us for rates for deliveries to remote or difficult areas so we could check whether we could meet the request. There is no sense in quoting a two hour rate and delivery to a location that is more than 140 miles from the pickup. We had another rate of $1.80 per loaded mile to locations not priced or not listed on our rate sheets. This rate was used during normal work hours, and we used higher rates for long runs after hours.

The underlying concept of the services offered and their pricing was to produce sustainable gross margins of at least 35 percent from on-demand activities.

Routed deliveries
Courier-routed work is priced in a different manner from on-

demand deliveries. Routed work usually cannot be combined with on-demand orders, so it must be priced at an hourly rate that will cover the costs of delivery, some overhead, and produce a reasonable profit margin. (Overhead is less because routed work has fewer time constraints and therefore requires less control over the driver.) Routed work usually must be profitable on its own because it often does not fit in with other work.

At Mid-Counties, we were fortunate to win a bid to run routes for a large title insurance company. We used as many as ten drivers a day. We provided the drivers and vehicles and the title company provided on-site supervision. We had this business for over ten years, and it was still in place when I sold the business. While our pricing for this type of business did not provide the upside potential available from on-demand work, we priced it to cover all the direct costs and a small amount of overhead and to provide a consistent margin of 20 percent, year after year. On-demand orders we received from this customer were not made by the route drivers.

Ordinarily, a company's quote to a potential customer for routed work is based on a daily or monthly amount, in spite of the fact that the detailed estimating should be done on an hourly basis. The hourly rate must be based on miles driven, time spent, and vehicle cost, just the same as for on-demand work.

Overnight deliveries

Overnight deliveries are not offered by every courier, because truckers and the national overnight services serve this market, with their low prices. Unless a courier is willing to look at overnight deliveries as "filler" business or has access to large vehicles to take advantage of large weight charges, he cannot make pickups and deliveries for as little as $15.00 or less, especially when the pickup and delivery may be 100 miles apart.

Some couriers attempt to make the overnight business profitable even if they do not have large vehicles with which to get weight charges on large loads by charging for weight at a rate of $.25 per pound or more. I believe this is a bad strategy unless the company services a small area. It is too hard to average $30.00 to $40.00 per hour from these small invoices, and without the big trucks, they never get the 10,000 pound loads to sweeten their averages.

Summary of Mid-Counties' Ground Charges		Minimum Charges	Miles Included
Service			
Same Day	Direct	$48.00	17.5
	2 Hour	$32.00	14.5
	4 Hour	$24.00	14.5
	6 Hour	$20.00	14.5
	8 Hour	$16.00	14.5
Overnight Express	within 40 miles	$16.00	
	within 60miles	$18.00	
	within 80 miles	$20.00	
	within 100 miles	$22.00	
Overnight Earlybird	Delivered by 10:00am	$20.00 added to base charge	
	Delivered by 9:00am	$30.00 added to base charge	
	Delivered by 8:00am	$40.00 added to base charge	
Overnight Latenight	within 50 miles	$26.00	
	75 miles	$28.00	
	within 100 miles	$30.00	

Additional Services

Additional services fall into two categories: those that are occasionally requested and those that occur because of an error on someone's part and are never requested.

Seldom requested services

Seldom requested services include picking up funds for customers (a type of C.O.D. delivery), insurance on cargo, two-person jobs, airport service, residential pickup or delivery, service to convention centers, service to military installations or school campuses, inside deliveries, lift gates, pallet jacks, document preparation, and surcharges for larger-than-standard vehicles and air ride vehicles.

Since these services are from time to time requested of all delivery companies, they should be carefully thought through and the price should appear on the rate sheet (and perhaps in the rating module of the company's computer system). Customer service should not be forced to compute the prices each time a request is received.

Several of these services warrant further comment. Some of the national overnight companies pick up checks but not cash. However, the shipper may not want a check from its customer and may have arranged for its customer to pay the delivering company with cash. DHL would not let its drivers accept payment of a C.O.D. with cash, so whenever such a request came to the DHL San Jose office, they either refused to make the delivery or turned it over to Mid-Counties. Mid-Counties deposited the cash in our bank account and paid DHL with one of our checks. The Mid-Counties operations people had to stay on top of the cash received from these deliveries, because if the drivers were not asked for these funds on returning to our office, they tended to "lose" them. Because of this exposure to loss, there must be a reasonable charge to pick up funds. We had a number of freight forwarder customers that complained when we charged for this C.O.D. service. Their position was that this service should be free or almost free since we were already charging them to go to the delivery location. We pointed out to them that we were exposed to the potential for a large loss from handling cash and checks, and therefore had to charge for this service.

Another service that must be priced properly is the charge for insurance on cargo transported. This service is a little tricky because a delivery company does not want to insure perishable product, works of art, or especially fragile product such as glass items. On the other hand, we have had customers who made everything from batteries to industrial equipment and would not give us the deliveries unless we could provide cargo insurance. When Mid-Counties was the only carrier involved in the pickup and delivery, we had a high level of confidence in our ability to safely transport the goods. However, when the shipment required that we use other carriers (including the airlines), we had to make sure that we had adequate insurance from each carrier that handled the cargo. We typically would not use a carrier that could not provide insurance on the cargo while the freight was in its control.

Our insurance coverage included the first $100 in value for all domestic shipments. If a customer required additional insurance, we priced it at the rate of $1.00 per $100 above the first $100 in declared value. This meant that a customer would pay $249 for additional insurance on cargo with a declared value of $25,000.

Insurance on international shipments generally must be priced higher, since little-known international carriers must be used and often collections cannot be made for losses sustained.

We had additional insurance charges as high as $2,000 and $3,000 each for local shipments for one customer who had incurred large losses from freight damaged by FedEx. This can be a great way for a company to increase its margins when its drivers are very careful with cargo. The operations department should alert the drivers about handling specific cargo with special precautions because of the additional insurance.

The additional insurance program must be coordinated with the insurance carrier, but in my experience, this does not cause insurance premiums to go up if losses are few and small. At Mid-Counties, when we received requests for additional insurance on large declared-value shipments (over $100,000), I usually informed the insurance agent in advance and attempted to get an approval before we accepted the freight. Also, on big-ticket items, we always inspected the equipment before it was packaged and then inspected it again after it was packaged or crated before we would accept the freight. If we did receive a claim for freight damage and there was no visible damage to the packaging, we denied the claim.

Never requested services
The prices for services that are never requested but which occur regularly should be clearly described in a company's rate sheet. These items include waiting time, attempted pickup or delivery, and wrong address. A clear policy on waiting time is mandatory for all delivery companies. Many customers have no compunction about requesting that a driver "stand by" for several hours while crating is completed or paperwork is prepared.

Probably the worst situation involving waiting time is in the delivery of show booths and advertising literature to trade shows. The large trade show facilities are ordinarily owned by cities, which generally support union services; so the movement of materials into and out of trade shows is generally contracted out to union managed services such as Greyhound. To make a delivery to a dock run by Greyhound employees, a delivery driver must drive to a dock where he is given a number and directed to a waiting lot that can be as much as 15 miles away. The driver is expected to remain in the lot until his number is called, usually between two and eight hours later. It is not unusual for the Greyhound employees to shut a dock down in mid-afternoon and expect the delivery drivers to return to their yard and come back the next morning to resume waiting. Once we had a driver who was forced to wait over 20 hours to make a delivery to the Moscone Center in San Francisco. Good luck in collecting a charge for something like that!

Freight forwarding and international remail
Pricing of freight forwarding and international remail services, where most of the cost comes from airlines and other carriers, is simple once the desired gross margin has been selected. The math is easy. If a company wants to make a gross margin of 20 percent, then it computes the sales price for a shipment costing $140.00 by simply dividing this number by .80, for the correct sales price of $175.00. However, selecting the appropriate gross margin percentage can be the tricky part. If a company is attempting to compete with run-of-the-mill, low cost freight forwarders that have large volumes and contract for guaranteed space with the airlines, a small company is lucky to get a 5 percent or 10 percent gross margin.

On the other hand, a much higher gross margin percentage is possible if a company can do any of the following:

- Provide expedited service, such as next available flight, and arrange for quick delivery when the freight arrives at its destination airport.

- Arrange complicated international shipments.

- Arrange international shipments to remote parts of countries such as India or certain parts of Arabic countries.

At Mid-Counties (MCD Air), we had developed or purchased deep knowledge of most aspects of the freight forwarding business, including developing many contacts with reliable delivery agents for our international shipments. These capabilities allowed us to average about 35 percent for gross margin on this segment of our business, and our freight forwarding business was our fastest growing division.

However, because of the uniqueness of these services, I was never satisfied with the margins we realized. I had an on-going battle with the manager of our freight forwarding division, because I was constantly trying to get him to charge an appropriate amount for complex transactions that took an inordinate amount of time. I wanted him to either keep track of the time we spent on each transaction and add it to our costs, or to increase the gross margin percentage toward 50 percent for the shipments where we provided superlative, unusual service. He apparently felt that realizing more than a 35 percent margin for this work was not fair to the customer.

Rate Sheet   From: Santa Cruz

Tariff Date: 8/31/02

		8-Hr Rate	4-Hr Rate	2-Hr Rate	Overnight
To	Alameda	$78.55	$117.80	$157.10	Call
To	Aptos	$16.00	$24.00	$32.00	$16.00
To	Aromas	$26.50	$39.75	$53.00	$16.00
To	Atherton	$49.95	$74.90	$99.90	$18.00
To	Belmont	$56.75	$85.15	$113.50	$18.00
To	Ben Lomond	$16.00	$24.00	$32.00	$16.00
To	Berkeley	$81.40	$122.10	$162.80	Call
To	Bonny Doon	$16.00	$24.00	$32.00	$16.00
To	Boulder Creek	$16.00	$24.00	$32.00	$16.00
To	Brisbane	$72.15	$108.25	$144.30	$20.00
To	Burlingame	$62.25	$93.40	$124.50	$20.00
To	Campbell	$27.70	$41.60	$55.45	$16.00
To	Capitola	$16.00	$24.00	$32.00	$16.00
To	Carmel	$50.80	$76.25	$101.65	$18.00
To	Castroville	$30.00	$45.00	$60.00	$16.00
To	Corralitos	$16.00	$24.00	$32.00	$16.00
To	Cupertino	$30.80	$46.20	$61.60	$16.00
To	Daly City	$75.15	$112.70	$150.25	Call
To	Davenport	$16.00	$24.00	$32.00	$16.00
To	Dublin	Call	Call	Call	Call
To	Emeryville	$79.20	$118.90	$158.40	Call
To	Felton	$16.00	$24.00	$32.00	$16.00
To	Foster City	$60.30	$90.40	$120.55	$20.00
To	Fremont	$52.00	$78.00	$104.00	$18.00
To	Gilroy	$46.30	$69.45	$92.60	$18.00
To	Half Moon Bay	Call	Call	Call	Call
To	Hayward	$61.60	$92.40	$123.20	$20.00
To	Hollister	$48.85	$73.25	$97.70	$18.00
To	Los Altos	$39.80	$59.75	$79.65	$16.00
To	Los Gatos	$21.90	$32.85	$43.80	$16.00
To	Marina	$36.95	$55.45	$73.90	$16.00
To	Menlo Park	$46.55	$69.80	$93.00	$18.00
To	Millbrae	$64.55	$96.85	$129.15	$18.00
To	Milpitas	$44.65	$67.00	$89.30	$16.00
To	Monterey	$45.45	$68.15	$90.85	$16.00
To	Morgan Hill	$53.35	$80.00	$106.70	$16.00
To	Moss Landing	$26.20	$39.25	$52.35	$16.00
To	Mountain View	$42.70	$64.00	$85.35	$16.00
To	Newark	$50.60	$75.90	$101.20	$18.00
To	Oakland	$77.75	$116.60	$155.50	Call
To	Pacific Grove	$52.80	$79.20	$105.60	$18.00

Rate Sheet

		8-Hr Rate	4-Hr Rate	2-Hr Rate	Overnight
To	Pacifica	$77.65	$116.50	$155.30	Call
To	Pajaro	$20.80	$31.20	$41.60	$16.00
To	Palo Alto	$43.35	$65.00	$86.70	$16.00
To	Pebble Beach	$50.00	$75.00	$100.00	$18.00
To	Prunedale	$35.55	$53.30	$71.00	$16.00
To	Redwood City	$51.15	$76.75	$102.30	$18.00
To	Salinas	$40.00	$60.00	$80.00	$16.00
To	San Carlos	$55.20	$82.85	$110.40	$18.00
To	San Francisco	$80.75	$121.10	$161.50	Call
To	San Jose	$33.20	$49.85	$66.40	$16.00
To	San Juan Baut.	$40.00	$60.00	$80.00	$16.00
To	San Leandro	$68.30	$102.50	$136.62	$20.00
To	San Lorenzo	$63.60	$95.40	$127.15	$18.00
To	San Martin	$61.25	$91.90	$122.50	$18.00
To	Santa Clara	$34.75	$52.15	$69.50	$16.00
To	Santa Cruz	$16.00	$24.00	$32.00	$16.00
To	Saratoga	$26.20	$39.30	$52.35	$16.00
To	Scotts Valley	$16.00	$24.00	$32.00	$16.00
To	Seaside	$43.80	$65.65	$57.55	$16.00
To	So San Francis	$70.00	$105.00	$140.00	$20.00
To	Soquel	$16.00	$24.00	$32.00	$16.00
To	Sunnyvale	$40.50	$60.70	$81.00	$16.00
To	Union City	$53.40	$81.50	$107.75	$18.00
To	Watsonville	$18.50	$27.70	$37.00	$16.00
To	Woodside	$48.60	$72.95	$97.25	$18.00

SERVICE RATES ARE BASED ON:

- 8-Hour Rate = $1.10 per mile, min $16.00
- 6-Hour Rate = $1.38 per mile, min $20.00
- 4-Hour Rate = $1.65 per mile, min $24.00
- 2-Hour Rate = $2.20 per mile, min $32.00
- Direct Rate = $2.75 per mile, min $48.00

Overnight Rates: (must be ready by 3:00 pm)
Pickup and delivered within 40 miles, $16.00
Pickup and delivered within 60 miles, $18.00
Pickup and delivered within 80 miles, $20.00
Pickup and delivered within 100 miles, $22.00
Beyond 100 miles, $1.80 per loaded mile

Latenight Rates: (must be ready by 8:00 pm)
Pickup and delivered within 50 miles, $26.00
Pickup and delivered within 75 miles, $28.00
Pickup and delivered beyond 75 miles, $30.00

WEIGHT CHARGES ARE:

```
   0 -   20 lbs -- no charge
  21 -  100 lbs -- $0.10 per pound
 101 - 1000 lbs -- $0.08 per pound
1001 - 2000 lbs -- $0.06 per pound
2001 - 4000 lbs -- $0.05 per pound
4001 - 6000 lbs -- $0.04 per pound
6001 - over     -- $0.035 per pound
```

General pricing assumes delivery using a standard delivery van. Deliveries requiring a cube van or bobtail will incur an added $25.00 charge.

All prices listed are estimates based on approximate distance between cities. Rates are subject to change at any time. Final prices will be based on current service rates, and actual distance and weight of each order.

Same Day Services

Deferred Services

8 Hour Same Day	Our most economical same day option. If your packages are ready by 10:00, we can deliver them by 6:00.
6 Hour Same Day	Packages must be ready by 11:30 for a delivery before 5:00 pm.
4 Hour Express	Packages must be ready by 12:30 for an express delivery within 4 hours.
2 Hour Express	Packages must be ready by 2:30 pm for an express delivery within 2 hours.
Direct Express	We dispatch the first available driver to pickup and deliver your shipment. This rate applies to time specific requests and all orders for pickups after 2:30 pm.

Packages must be ready by 3:00 for next business day delivery before noon. See Overnight Specials for earlier delivery options.	**Overnight Express**
We can pick up packages until 8:00 pm for a next business day delivery by noon. See Overnight Specials for earlier deliver options.	**Overnight Late night**
MCD also provides "Less Than Truckload" shipping services. Call today for more information.	**LTL Ground**
Our Next Flight service offers the fastest alternative for critical deliveries over longer distances.	**Next Flight**
MCD Air provides domestic and international forwarding worldwide, and Domestic Express and International Express services. Call for pricing and capabilities.	**Air Freight**

SAME DAY SERVICE AVAILABILITY
(Refer to rate sheets for actual pricing)

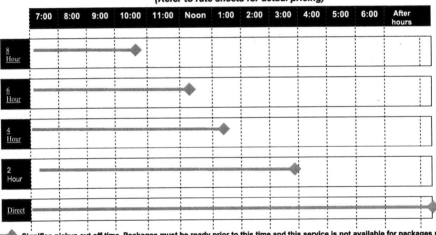

➤ Signifies pickup cut off time. Packages must be ready prior to this time and this service is not available for packages ready after this time.

❑ **ADDITIONAL SERVICES**:
✓ C.O.D. - $10
✓ Proof of Delivery - $1 US Mail or Fax, and $1.50 for ea additional request
✓ Waiting Time - $7 for each 10 minutes after first 10 minutes
✓ Each domestic shipment insured for $100. Added ins is $1 per $100 in declared value. Call for international shipping insurance rates.
✓ Airport service - $10
✓ Rural residential delivery or pickup - $10 if under 100 lbs, $20 if over 100 lbs
✓ Wrong address - $10
✓ Convention Centers - $20 plus waiting time
✓ School campuses and Military installations - $10
✓ Attempted pickups - half rate
✓ Inside delivery - $10 plus $.03 per pound
✓ Lift gate, pallet jack - $20
✓ Off hours surcharge for service between 11pm and 7am, Mon thru Fri, after 7pm Sat, after 5pm Sun, and all day on holidays - $50
✓ 2-man jobs - $40/hr/extra man. Minimum: $40
✓ Document preparation - $5

❑ **OVERNIGHT SPECIALS**:
✓ Early Bird Deliveries of Overnight services only:
  ▪ For delivery by 8:00am, add $40
  ▪ For delivery by 9:00am, add $30
  ▪ For delivery by 10:00am add $20

❑ **SECURED WAREHOUSING – CALL FOR RATES**

❑ **SPECIAL CONTRACT RATES – CALL FOR RATES**

❑ **INTERNATIONAL REMAIL – CALL FOR RATES**

❑ **RESTRICTIONS**:
✓ Rates apply to services Mon – Fri between 7 am and 6 pm
✓ 2-Hr Express rates apply to services on Sat from 8 am to 4
✓ Direct Express rates apply to services after 2:30pm week Sat, and all day Sun and Holidays. Designated pickup o delivery times will also cause Direct Express rates to apply
✓ Weights subject to dimensional charges – dim factor 194

Business	Monday through Friday,	7:00 am – 11:00 pm	(All rates apply depending on time availability)
	Saturday	8:00 am – 4:00 pm	(2-hour & Direct Express rates available)
Hours:	After Hours, Sundays, Holidays	on call	(Direct Express rates available)

Costs |6|

Subjects covered in this chapter
- *Direct, indirect, variable, and fixed costs*
- *Controlling costs and the role of a good chart of accounts*

The ability of any business to survive, let alone prosper, depends largely on management's understanding of the company's costs. The business of on-demand deliveries is like the construction industry, in that each delivery is a separate, fixed-fee job with a very short time-to-completion, and management must endeavor to make each job (delivery) profitable on its own. In order to ensure that each job has a chance to be profitable, someone in the company must understand all the elements of cost. If rates have been established based on a good understanding of costs, and if the company has a system for tightly managing its drivers, then each job priced from the rate sheet should be profitable. In addition, if customer service reps are equipped with cost information for work by the day, by the hour, by the mile, and by vehicles of various sizes, quotes can be made quickly for work that is not off the rate sheet, with the assurance that the work will be profitable.

Direct Costs

The first costs to be fully understood are the costs of making the pickup and delivery. Since a driver in a vehicle ordinarily makes a delivery, these costs, in relation to revenue, determine whether enough gross margin (profit) is produced by the job. The costs of drivers and vehicles are directly related to the revenue they produce and are termed **"direct costs."** Other costs, such as dispatching, order taking, billing, etc. are not directly related to specific jobs and are called **"indirect costs."** In order to calculate gross margin, direct costs and certain indirect costs should be deducted from revenue. Indirect costs not reflected against revenue, such as selling and administrative costs, are generally called **"expenses."** This terminology and grouping of costs can best be seen on the income statement shown on page 33.

Since most direct costs vary directly with the revenue they produce, some like to call these "variable" costs. In truth, however, some direct costs do not vary in relation to revenue. These costs, such as rent, depreciation, and to some extent insurance, are "fixed" costs. There is quite a distinction between direct / indirect costs and variable / fixed costs, and these terms should not be used interchangeably.

Direct driver costs

Drivers are usually paid on an hourly basis, so the costs of drivers are ordinarily thought of in terms of so much per hour. However, quotes for new work must often be made in terms of monthly or weekly amounts. In order to do this quickly, the following conversions should be committed to memory:

Work hours per week	40
Work hours per year— 40 hours X 52 weeks	2080
Work hours per month— 2080 / 12 months	173

The cost of a driver, however, is more than his hourly or monthly pay. Payroll taxes in California add about 10 percent to an employee's pay for social security, medicare, federal unemployment, and state disability. These payroll taxes seem to be ever increasing; the specific amounts can be easily obtained from a company's current payroll. Workers' compensation in California for a driver currently dictates a base rate of over 20 percent of a driver's pay. This rate can go up or down depending on a company's experience modification factor, which is based on the number of workers' comp claims and the dollar amount of the claims during three of the last four years. Payroll benefits and workers' compensation are mandatory, and if a company provides no other fringe benefits to its drivers, then the hourly cost of a driver is the hourly pay rate plus at least 30 percent. As you can see, a $10 an hour person really costs $13.00 an hour or more.

Over the years, many delivery companies and couriers have begun paying additional, discretionary fringe benefits in order to attract and retain good drivers. These discretionary benefits can add a total of 15 percent or more to a company's fringe benefit rate:

- Two weeks vacation - 3.85 percent (80hrs / 2080hrs)
- One week's sick pay - 1.92 percent (40hrs / 2080hrs)
- Seven days' vacation pay - 2.69 percent (56hrs / 2080hrs)
- Medical / dental costs - (at $50 to $500 a month per employee, $100 for a $10 per hour employee,- 5.78 percent ($100 / [$10 x 173hrs])
- 401k plan - 1 to 3 percent

A $10.00 an hour pay rate becomes a lot closer to $15.00 by the time all the fringes are added. At Mid-Counties, we used $15.00 an hour or $120.00 per day as driver costs for budgetary purposes or for quoting new work.

Typically, larger companies provide more generous benefits. As they begin providing medical and dental coverage for dependants, extended vacation and sick leave, educational benefits, etc., the benefits rate can be anywhere from 50 percent to 75 percent of base pay. Therefore, on strictly a cost basis, Federal Express, Airborne, UPS, DHL, and even national same day companies that use their own drivers will not be able to compete with a local courier or trucker for local same day work because most local companies do not pay all these extended benefits. In my opinion, this cost advantage, when combined with excellent service, provides a market niche for same day deliveries that will not soon be lost to the national companies.

Direct vehicle costs

Vehicle costs are usually the second largest expense for a delivery company, behind only employee wages and benefits. Since about 15 percent of every revenue dollar is spent on a company's vehicles, it is certainly worthwhile to pay attention to this expense classification.

The IRS provides a good guide for vehicle costs by allowing an employee to be reimbursed for using a personal vehicle for work at the rate (for 2005) of $.405 per mile. If the employee is reimbursed at a higher rate, the excess must be included as earnings by the employee and taxes paid on it, or the employee must be able to prove his costs are more than the allowable amount if he is audited. At Mid-Counties, when the IRS reimbursement rate was lower, we used $.325 per mile as our standard vehicle cost for pickup trucks and other small vehicles, $.35 per mile for vans, and $.50 per mile for bobtails. In 2005, if a driver averaged 250 miles a day in a small vehicle, the actual vehicle cost would be approximately $101.00 a day.

The proof of the pudding as far as vehicle costs are concerned is to do an annual check of actual vehicle costs per mile. (All vehicle costs should be recorded in a separate numeric series. See the chart of accounts listed at page 21 to 30.) This is done by dividing the vehicle costs captured by the accounting system by the total number of miles driven during the year. By making this annual calculation at Mid-Counties, we have found that our vehicle costs typically fell into a range of $.29 to $.33 per mile. The detailed vehicle costs included in our calculation included fuel, mileage reimbursement, maintenance, repairs, parts, washing, registration, tires, rentals, smog permits, physical damage, towing, depreciation, and insurance.

We kept track of each driver's time and mileage each day (recorded on the driver's log), and our drivers had for years averaged approximately 300 miles per day. So, we knew that our direct costs ran $120 a day for drivers ($15 x 8hrs) and about $100 per day for vehicles ($.33 x 300 miles), or $220 for the driver and a vehicle. This works out to a direct cost of $27.50 per hour.

When I bought Mid-Counties, the company's vehicles consisted mainly of mini-pickups with camper shells. My first vehicle purchases were made solely on the basis of price. In those days, I could buy small trucks for as little as $5,500 each. My philosophy regarding vehicles has always been to drive them until they began to develop a pattern of recurring breakdowns. Since I bought the least expensive vehicles available, I found I needed to have them fully paid for in three years. We found that, on average, we drove our trucks 60,000 miles per year, and most of the little pickups were pretty much worn out after three years. Every once in a while, however, we would get a mini-pickup that would be operable with few problems for 300,000 to 350,000 miles. This meant that for these long-lived vehicles with average costs of upkeep, I was able to skip the purchase on one new vehicle by driving the old truck twice as long.

As the freight we hauled became larger, we were forced to buy larger, more expensive vehicles. We first moved to mini-vans, but soon realized that we could get more pallets into a full size van or even an extended van. Although the vans cost at least twice as much as the little pickups, maintenance costs were about the same, gas mileage was only a little worse, we averaged almost twice as many miles on the vans as on the pickups, and each van was capable of bringing in much more revenue than the little pickups. The vans seemed to operate dependably until they had about 300,000 miles on them, and we would get the odd van that was good for 400,000 plus miles.

This pattern of larger loads and larger trucks continued, and we began to buy package vans and then bobtails. With the larger package vans and bobtails, I bought a few diesels and found these engines to be more reliable than comparable gasoline engines; however, they were 15 percent to 20 percent more expensive.

As our vehicle fleet grew with the addition of the larger trucks, I found that we had more fully depreciated trucks on the books. (I always used a five-year life and straight-line depreciation for book purposes—although we used accelerated depreciation for tax purposes.) Even with these larger vehicles, our maintenance costs were only slightly higher than they had been with the smaller trucks. I could see that if I had stayed in the business, we would have reached the point where the majority of our vehicles were fully depreciated but still usable. This would have been a nice cost reduction (a $40,000 truck costs $8,000 a year in straight-line depreciation over five years). Depreciation, in my opinion, is sort of a benign cost, because once you have made the decision to buy a vehicle, the monthly depreciation does not seem so high. It is only when you look at annual depreciation in relation to net income that you get the full impact of depreciation's effect on costs. In the final years of my ownership of Mid-Counties, I concluded that it was better to buy vehicles that had a reputation for long life, even if it meant paying more for them, than to buy less costly vehicles. It is a very nice feeling to have fully paid for and fully depreciated vehicles in your fleet. Also, this puts the company in a flexible position if the economy slows down, because the only fixed costs associated with fully paid for and depreciated vehicles are their annual registration costs and their permits to use the roads.

At Mid-Counties, we used a mobile mechanic who came to our facility during the week when we had major work to be done. This person handled minor repairs and oil changes on the weekends when most of the vehicles were in the yard. We scheduled oil changes every 3,000 to 5,000 miles, and felt that this activity was crucial for long engine life.

One of the ongoing problems with the operation of a fleet is the system of providing fuel. Since drivers never seem to carry cash or credit cards, the company has to either have numerous fuel stations available in their service area with a permanent credit card on file, or each vehicle must have a credit card assigned to it that can be used at any service station of a certain brand.

At Mid-Counties, we used both of these systems and caught drivers using the company's credit cards to fill their personal vehicles with both systems. For the stations where we had a single card on file for use by any Mid-Counties driver, we provided the stations with written instructions that stated the fuel purchased had to be pumped into a vehicle that bore the Mid-Counties logo. This worked at some stations, but in others the drivers made friends with the station clerks and seemed to have no trouble convincing the clerks to let them fill up their personal vehicles and mark the charge slips as if the purchase were for the company truck.

A sales person convinced me that it would be better to have a card assigned to a specific vehicle to be used at various stations in the area. We used this system with a number of our vehicles that had small gas tanks, because the drivers complained they could not always get back to the station where they had credit privileges before they ran out of gas. I thought this system was working well until we started getting charges signed for by drivers after they had left the company. I finally had to completely do away with this system.

I would hate to guess how much gasoline drivers stole over the years, but this is another reason I was migrating toward diesel for the entire Mid-Counties' fleet.

Some companies let their drivers take vehicles home in the evening, and unless the vehicle is a 40-foot tractor-trailer, you can count on the driver and his family using the vehicle for everything from going shopping to driving across the state to visit relatives on the weekend. If the company has a global positioning system to track these vehicles at all hours of the day and night, it can be very discouraging to see how many non-business miles are put on them. And even worse, they are often involved in off-duty accidents. I recommend that all vehicles be returned to the yard every evening.

Indirect Costs

While direct costs can be tied to invoices that are generated because of the work of the drivers, this relationship is not meaningful for indirect costs. When drivers do not have enough work to keep them busy, they are generally sent home. Operations management, order taking, dispatching and often billing must carry on even when some drivers are not needed. These costs are called indirect, and because they are incurred mainly to assist the drivers with the daily activities of making pickups and deliveries, they are deducted from revenues along with the direct costs to generate the company's gross margin.

Other indirect costs are even less connected to the daily activities of making pickups and deliveries. These costs, which include selling, marketing, accounting, and general management, are called "expenses," and on a statement of operations are deducted from gross margin to produce income before taxes.

Controlling Costs

Many aids exist to help control and manage costs, although most seem to be directed toward managing the drivers. These aids include:

- Background checks on prospective employees
- Time clocks or software to make sure employees are working when they are supposed to be
- Daily driver logs that track the time of every stop and its purpose
- Voice and data communication devices and systems
- Global positioning systems to check vehicle locations and speeds
- Very effective systems for rating orders, dispatching, billing, communicating with customers, collecting slow accounts, etc.

In addition to the above systems, a financial control that every company should install is a system of **departmental cost centers.** As a bare minimum, a company should capture its direct costs in a department, its indirect operating costs in a department and its expenses in at least two departments—administration and sales & marketing. The chart of accounts holds this departmental system together. It is very important in managing the overall profitability of the enterprise. In spite of the systems that allow a company to micro-manage every detail of a driver's day, at the end of the day, or the week, or the month, management needs to know that the drivers and vehicles cost the company no more than 50 to 60 percent of the revenues they generated. Management also needs to know that the company's other operational costs were no more than 20 percent of revenues, and that sales and administration combined were no more than 15 percent of revenues. This information is produced by the departmental reports. As a company grows, it is very difficult to manage overall profitability without a good breakout of costs by functional department. A sample chart of accounts that allows for this type of control is shown on page 21 to 30.

The terminologies mentioned above, as well as departmental cost centers, are used universally, so published financial statements for any public company contain numbers and notes to the financial statements based on departmental classifications, often described in terms of fixed, variable, direct, or indirect costs.

Another Way of Looking at Delivery Costs | 7 |

Subjects covered in this chapter
- *Comparing costs for a company that uses its own employees vs. one that uses independent contractors*
- *Rules for determining if a worker meets the independent contractor criteria*
- *How many employees a company can afford*

Fifteen years ago, when I got into the delivery business by buying a company, pricing was dictated by couriers and delivery companies that used independent contractors in place of employees. At that time, a company would hire a driver who owned a vehicle and would pay this person a commission of between 45 to 60 percent of the revenues he or she produced. This commission compensated the driver for his time plus the use of his vehicle. If the driver was considered an independent contractor, the company had no liability for workers' compensation insurance or the employer's portion of payroll taxes. And since the contractor owned the vehicle, the company was not responsible for comprehensive and collision vehicle insurance.

This is a very good system for a company because it just about guarantees that each job will produce a high gross margin, since the company does not pay for the time drivers are lost, driver breaks or long lunches, overtime pay, holiday pay, sick pay, vehicle maintenance, or accident costs. And with no vehicles, the company does not have to worry about stolen gasoline and oil.

For example, if a company considers its drivers independent contractors and compensates them by means of a 50 percent commission, then the operating statements of the company will be something like the following:

	With Independent Contractors	With Employees
Revenue	100 %	100 %
Less- Direct costs of deliveries	50 %	65 %
Revenue less direct costs	50 %	35 %
Less-Dispatch & other operating costs	15 %	15 %
Gross margin	35 %	20 %
Less- Expenses:		
Selling	10 %	6 %
General & administrative	6 %	5 %
Interest	4 %	4 %
Total expenses	20 %	15 %
Profit before taxes	15 %	5 %

The beauty of this system is that the delivery costs vary directly in relationship to revenues. This makes profitability easier to control and more consistent than when drivers are paid by the hour and the company owns the vehicles.

The Way the Government Wants It

In California and other states, the Internal Revenue Service and the Economic Development Department aggressively attempt to ensure that companies in the transportation business provide the federal and state governments with the enormous sums of money they require to operate. This means that in California, these regulatory bodies attempt to make sure that all workers are paid as employees rather than independent contractors, that they are paid at least minimum wage, that overtime hours are paid at the higher of the state or the federal rates, and that drivers who use their own vehicles do not get a high vehicle reimbursement rate and a pay rate lower than the minimum wage after calculating overtime based on the statutory rates. Therefore, the IRS and EDD need to ensure that compensation is reported as payroll so payroll taxes and workers' comp collections are as high as possible.

If a company does not want to risk a hefty fine from the IRS and the EDD, it must follow these rules to the letter. This usually means that driver's pay, including benefits, will be higher than if the drivers were compensated as independent contractors, and if the company provides the vehicles, then its vehicle costs will also be higher than if the independent contractors owned them.

If a company must pay its drivers by the hour as employees, it should set its pay rates so that driver payroll costs—which should include a percentage for benefits—are no more than 35 percent of the average revenues brought in by the drivers. If revenue per driver averages $250 per day, and if drivers do not work overtime, then driver's pay with benefits could be $250/8 = $31.25 X .35 = $11.00 per hour, generating an acceptable gross margin. If drivers work an average of 1.0 hours of overtime at time and one half to generate their daily revenues, then the appropriate pay rate changes to $250/9.5 = $26.32 X .35 = $9.20 per hour. As you can see, each hour of overtime is incredibly expensive to the company. In order to keep the same 35 percent relationship between revenues and burdened driver pay (and correspondingly the same gross margin percentage), that hour of overtime should have brought in approximately $47.00. This is an example of why deliveries outside the normal workday must be priced so high.

Besides the hourly pay to drivers, there are fringe benefit costs that include the company's portion of payroll taxes, vacation pay, sick pay, workers' comp costs, and 401k costs. If a company is especially generous, driver's costs can easily creep up to 50 to 55 percent of revenues, unless delivery rates are also increased. So, every time workers' comp rates increase, or a company's payroll tax rates change, or medical insurance rates increase, delivery rates need to be increased. Delivery rates must be increased every year. And if some other cost such as fuel suddenly increases significantly, then a surcharge or mid-year rate increase should occur.

In my experience, vehicle costs for a delivery service are typically budgeted at 10 to 15 percent of revenues. But when the economy slows down and a company finds itself with more vehicles than it needs, or when the economy is good and a company must hire and train new drivers who are involved in numerous accidents, then vehicle costs can easily increase to 20 percent of revenues or more.

Therefore, when drivers are employees and the company owns the vehicles, it is easy for the direct costs of making deliveries to exceed 75 percent of revenues. Because of this, I believe that it is always preferable to use independent contractors rather than employees. However, if a company uses independent contractors and is audited and cannot justify the independent contractors classification, the legal fees for fighting the IRS or EDD can put a company out of business. And this is without the penalties and interest that are certain to be assessed. This is why at Mid-Counties, I always had employees rather than independent contractors. I could not justify the risk, even though with independent contractors it certainly is easier to make profits.

As you can see, when drivers are employees and the company owns the vehicles, the company assumes all the operating risks, with limited possibilities of having the occasional extraordinarily good year to offset the bad ones. Management, then, must constantly and quickly react to the hundreds of variables that are for the most part out of their control and which almost always change in a way to decrease the company's profits.

The Current Trend

I should mention that when the economy began to slow down in 2000, many delivery companies were forced to consider the independent contractor or owner/operator classification for its drivers or be forced out of business. A number of firms throughout the U.S. handle the contracts and other paperwork for the reclassification of employees as independent contractors. These companies typically put the independent contractors on their own payroll and handle billing the company, vehicle insurance, workers' comp insurance (if the independent contractor wants it), medical insurance, retirement programs, and various other programs and activities. They maintain legal staffs to fight challenges by the IRS and EDD and apparently have been successful in defending the independent contractor classification in most states.

What Are Independent Contractors?

If a company is considering a reclassification of its employees to independent contractors, it should review the EDD Employment Determination Guide, _www.edd.ca.gov/taxrep/de38.pdf_, and the June 2003 IRS Form SS-8, _www.irs.gov/pub/irs-pdf_/fss8.pdf, to get the EDD and IRS thinking on proper classification.

Listed below are factors that should be considered in determining if a worker meets the owner/operator (independent contractor) criteria. The more factors that fit, the better the chance that "independent contractor" is the correct classification.

- The company has no right to control the manner and means of how the contractor accomplishes the results desired, regardless of whether that right is actually exercised. (This is probably the most important factor.)
- The contractor acts like a separate business (i.e., equity, contracts, invoices, leases, insurance, employees, etc.).
- The contractor is in a distinct occupation or separate business. (The contractor should have his or her own business license or operating permit.)
- The contractor uses personal tools and assets (vehicles).
- The contractor is highly skilled, works without supervision of the company and uses initiative, judgment and foresight for success of the independent operation.
- The parties believe they are creating a principal—independent contractor relationship.
- The contractor has the right to hire and discharge others.
- The contractor does not have a company title or business card.
- The contractor's work is not the company's primary work.
- The contractor has financial control of the business (i.e., significant investment in the business, opportunity for profit or loss, and pays own expenses).
- The contractor decides where the work is to be done and sets his or her own hours.

- The contractor is paid by the job.
- The contractor's relationship is short-term.
- The contractor cannot be terminated at will.

How Many Employees Should a Company Have?

In considering gross margins, keep in mind that unless a company does some freight forwarding or generates quite a bit of revenue from warehousing, the drivers are the key to profitability. While one driver producing a gross margin of 40 percent every day may be able to support an accounts payable clerk, if the driver produces a daily gross margin of 25 percent or less, it takes several drivers to fund even the most inexpensive support employee. For sales personnel or managers, it can take six or more drivers to support one person. A delivery company with ten drivers averaging $250 per day in revenues will have annual revenues of over $600,000, but it probably will not be able to afford a salesman or an experienced operations person. The owner will have to handle most of those chores. A company that does $1,500,000 a year in revenues should have only four or five employees other than its 20 to 25 drivers.

Cash Flow $\boxed{8}$

Subjects covered in this chapter
- *Third party payment companies*
- *Tips on how to collect receivables*
- *Ways to reduce bad debt write-offs*

One of the greatest problems for any small company is cash management. An owner is always fighting the battle of covering payrolls and paying bills. For a delivery company, cash flow will usually be a problem, because this segment of the transportation industry is extremely competitive. Anyone who has a bike, a car, or a pickup is a potential competitor. All this competition keeps prices low and margins thin. Stiff competition is not limited to small companies. Once when we were negotiating a new contract with DHL, the station manager mentioned that DHL was a "2 percent company," which was his way of letting me know that he expected me to keep my prices to DHL low.

Transportation companies that use their own employees to make deliveries can expect to pay half of the company's revenues to the employees as payroll and payroll taxes. This means that every two weeks, the employees will be paid 50 percent of the previous two weeks' revenue, even though most of the customers will not pay for the work until 30 to 60 days after they have been billed. Companies that use a delivery service for repeat business expect it to grant them credit in the form of their own account, with terms of "payment due on receipt" or "net 10 days", but very few customers honor these terms.

The Business Relationship

When I was a financial officer for several manufacturing companies in Silicon Valley, I developed special relationships with the accounts payable people of our major customers, who knew that, while we were a small company, we provided a critical product to them. As a result, we could call them for a check on short notice if the need arose. I was not able to develop these relationships with any of my large customers in the transportation industry.

At Mid-Counties, we did a lot of our business with large semiconductor companies and software companies, but it was virtually impossible to get a check from them on short notice. Most large high tech companies do not pay their transportation vendors themselves. They have outsourced this to third party payment services, which are usually located in another part of the country (or now, the world).

These payment services (such as NPC, Berman and Blake, NTA, AIM, Pay Tech, Cor Pay Solutions, and Software Solutions) are used because they slow down the payment cycle by seldom paying before 45 days from billing date. They search out missing details on invoices such as authorization numbers, misspelled names, and department codes, which must be corrected before payment will be made. They can put a hold on payments because of a delivery address they do not recognize or a rate they cannot figure out. They almost never call the delivery service for information. Instead, they put a hold on the invoice and send it to the delivery company's customer for resolution. This generally adds three weeks to the payment time. The delivery service is not the customer of these invoice payers, so the payers do not care if the service ever gets its money. Even after the invoices have been checked, approved, and placed in a batch for payment, a check will not be cut until the bill payer has funds in its checking account from the customer. If the customer wires funds to the bill payer, a check can be cut and released the same week. However, if the customer sends a check, the bill payer waits until the check has been deposited and the funds are in its bank account before it begins the process of writing a check to the delivery service. This also can easily be a three-week process.

Several years ago, the "San Jose Mercury News" ran an article on the enormous cash balances enjoyed by the large semiconductor companies in Silicon Valley. The company with the most cash, of course, was Intel, with something like $8 billion in cash and marketable securities on its balance sheet. We had done a little work for Intel for six or seven years. We picked up at one of their vendors several times a week and delivered that same day to another. Intel always used a third party payment company, so they never paid us promptly; however, the amounts were not large and we were appreciative of the work they gave us. A year or so before I sold Mid-Counties, Intel, with much correspondence and documentation, changed third party payment companies, and our cash receipts came to a halt. It took approximately six months to get the funds flowing again and involved countless telephone calls to anyone who would listen to our plight. This situation occurs because no one at these large companies is actually responsible for making sure vendors get paid.

It is a sad situation when companies separate themselves from their vendors by outsourcing a function as important as paying bills. Aside from causing pain and misery for the vendors, it severs possibly the most critical relationship between the two companies. Cash is the life-blood of any business, and after all, if the delivery company cannot pay its employees and vendors in a timely fashion, why even do the work?

Spreading the Risk

Another feature of cash flow is spreading the risk of failure to pay or slow pay by the customers. Ideally, a company would not have more than 10 percent of its accounts receivable from a single customer. However, everything else being equal, companies should take whatever profitable business is available to them when it fits their business model. If this results in one large customer that dominates a delivery company's activities, the company can only direct its sales efforts to try to acquire more business, so no one customer exposes the company to bankruptcy.

In our customer base, I was dismayed by the fact that at one time Intel, NEC, Lockheed, The Santa Cruz Operation, Cisco, and Seagate all used the same bill paying company. From a cash standpoint, these businesses were almost like one account to us, since all their payments came from one distant, invisible, disinterested entity.

A Program to Generate Cash

Managing cash flow should be a more established program than simply making telephone calls occasionally and hoping for the best. Many customers have their own programs to not pay in accordance with their vendors' stated payment terms, so a delivery service must be at least as aggressive and smart as its customers in order to collect accounts receivable within an acceptable period of time.

Over the years, we developed the following program to collect receivables. While we never seemed to have much cash on our balance sheet, this collection program eliminated some of the sleepless nights I inherited when I first bought the company.

Companies that ask for a credit account so they can begin using your services are told that you require payment in advance for the first order by check or cash, and that an account will be opened for subsequent orders. This keeps incidental and one-time users, and even some low volume accounts, on a cash basis. In addition to providing a little cash up front, the program will greatly reduce collection efforts. Further, your bad debt expense will drop, because it is very difficult to collect small balances under $50. (Collection agencies do not like small balances, because they take as much time and effort to collect as a large balance without providing much revenue.) We set up our "Cash" accounts receivable account so we would not have to open a separate account for each cash-basis customer. It was always in our Top 25 Accounts by Revenue list. Because of this way we handled new accounts, we often did not ask for credit information before we started work for a new customer.

For new customers outside our service area that did not have an account and were unable to get a check to us before we did the work, we would work on credit if they agreed to mail a check to us immediately. We charged these amounts to a "Miscellaneous" account and sent them our standard bill of lading as their invoice instead of opening a separate account for them. This type of request came mainly from freight forwarders outside our area. In spite of their promises to pay, amounts charged to our Miscellaneous accounts receivable were slow to pay and hard to collect, mainly because our charge was a one-time event and our billing was often an exception to their normal recurring vendor activities. Our Miscellaneous accounts receivable took a lot of collection work and was a major contributor to our bad debt expense. Even so, I consider this a cost-justified, effective procedure.

We never accepted payment by credit card because I believed credit cards encouraged individuals rather than businesses to use our service. I found dealing with individuals and the resultant residential deliveries to be generally unprofitable. In fact, we charged an extra $10.00 for a residential pickup or delivery, though I doubt this was enough, since we often could not pickup or leave a package if no one was home. Also, individuals often requested a pickup or delivery at a specific time when someone was expected to be home. This was a very expensive situation, since the driver had to interrupt his normal schedule to be at the location at a certain time. And, of course, we almost never had a chance to consolidate the residential pickup or delivery with other deliveries nearby. This is why deliveries or pickups at an exact time should be priced at a company's most expensive same day rate.

The number of bounced checks we received from our corporate customers each year was very low, one or two checks a year at most. In the unusual situation when we did receive an NSF check from a corporate customer, we simply redeposited it, and in 99 percent of the cases, the check cleared. In dealing with individuals, however, our experience was that once a check bounced, it usually bounced a second time. At that point, we were faced with trying to obtain cash from the person, which takes a lot of time and effort. This is another reason why I found dealing with individuals unprofitable.

Billings should be done at least weekly and should generally occur on the same day each week. Businesses are accustomed to weekly invoices from UPS and daily invoices from Federal Express, so they will accept weekly billing from another delivery service with no questions. Some small accounts may be billed monthly to satisfy a customer.

At Mid-Counties, we wanted the billing date to be the date we made the pickup, not the date of delivery. This meant that if we had work that was not delivered the same day we made the pickup (such as an overnight delivery, a 2-3 day delivery, or airfreight), we may have needed several days after the end of our billing period to obtain and enter proof of delivery information. Our workweek was Monday through Sunday, and we generally got our bills out late Tuesday or Wednesday. By following this scheme of billing, because so much of our work was overnight, we generally moved as much as 10 percent of our receivables up one week. And that, in turn, resulted in cash coming in a week earlier.

Terms on a delivery company's invoice should require payment upon receipt and provide for the right to charge interest on balances older than 30 days. Our invoices stated "*Payment due on receipt. Past due accounts are subject to a service charge of 2 percent per month including interest, which is an annual payment rate of 24 percent.*" While it is unusual in the transportation industry to charge interest on old accounts receivable balances (Federal Express, DHL, Airborne Express, the airlines, and most truckers do not charge interest on past due balances), Mid-Counties began charging a service charge a few years ago. We made the calculations and posted the charges monthly during the week that included the last day of the month. However, we did not pick up the interest as revenue. Instead, we credited a deferred revenue account in the current liability section of the balance sheet, and we only transferred the deferred revenue to the income statement when an amount had been paid. While none of our customers liked a finance charge for a late payment, some would pay it and many would pay sooner so the charge would not appear on their bill. It takes a little effort to keep track of the balance in the deferred revenue account, but I believe this program was very effective and one of our main tools in helping to collect cash.

Many large customers regularly invite delivery services to participate in a Request for Quotation (RFQ) procedure every year or two. While many indicate service level as their major criterion for selection, I have found that low price is usually their main interest, and the work usually goes to the low bidder. If a delivery company wins the business as the result of an RFQ, it is required to sign a contract that clearly spells out the low prices. It is the delivery service's responsibility to make sure the contract provides for payment of its invoices in accordance with the terms necessary to provide the low prices.

I have found over the years that it is not enough to merely have a contract specify payment within a certain number of days after the work is invoiced. As discussed above, the largest companies in my area did not themselves make the payments. This function was outsourced to a third party. So, although a delivery company may be providing services in accordance with the contract, the customer almost never will meet its obligation for timely contracted payments. Even when the customer is 60 to 90 days behind in his payments, the problem always seems to be blamed on the third party payer and outside the control of the customer. Without some other provision in the contract, the only solution for the delivery service is to grin and bear it, or stop doing work for this customer until it gets paid. Of course, if work is stopped for the customer, that business is in jeopardy, as well as any long-term relationship with that customer. As a practical matter, UPS and Federal Express can take dramatic measures like this with customers, but a small delivery service generally cannot, even if the customer's failure to pay has taken it right up to the point of bankruptcy.

A delivery service must expect companies that use third party payers to fail to make payments in accordance with the agreement, and therefore a penalty provision for failure to pay on time should be spelled out in the contract. If the payment terms are "net 30," the contract should state that for charges older than either 45 days or 60 days, the carrier is permitted to charge interest on the past due balance. The payment terms on the carrier's invoice must also state that past due amounts over the same period will incur a service charge at some fairly high rate. The rates on the contract and on the invoice should be the same. A fair monthly interest rate for amounts 45 days past due is 1.5 percent, and for 60 days, 2 percent. As stated above, while only a few companies actually paid the interest charge when it was invoiced, most did not like to see it on their bill and paid faster because of it.

In addition to our contractual right to bill and collect an interest charge after 60 days, our contracts provided that after 90 days, the customer lost its discount and we could increase the amount of the discounted, 90 days past due charges to our published rates, as well as charge published rates for any new work.. When we notified their traffic departments of these facts after the 90 days, their finance departments were brought into a meeting, and we were always paid.

In addition to all the measures taken before any work is done for new customers and new contracts, every delivery service must have someone make collection calls each week. At Mid-Counties, we generally called on balances over 40 days old and asked for payment or for a commitment on a date when a check was to be released.

For non-contract customers with past due balances, we used a separate two-part program to collect amounts more than 60 days past due. We used a collection system that consisted of a series of dunning letters, followed by actually turning the creditors over to a collection agency. A collection company mailed a series of five dunning letters on their letterhead. The letters were increasingly firm. The last letter was very nasty and stated that the account was about to be turned over to a collection agency that was prepared to take the matter to court. We generally received payment before the account was actually turned over to the collection agency. We paid $10 for each series of five letters rather than paying collection fees on the amounts collected as a result of the letters.

Occasionally, the letters were not successful and an account was actually turned over to the collection agency. We found that if the balance was $250 or over, the collection agency was very interested in collecting the amount (since their fee was 50 percent of any amount collected), and they did a thorough job. They were not as interested in smaller balances, which caused a lot of our bad debt expense.

If we consistently had trouble collecting from an account, we revoked their credit privileges and required they pay in advance for any work we did. We had a handful of accounts that had lost their credit privileges and still used us.

Measuring the Effectiveness of a Cash Collection Program

The proof of whether or not a cash collection program is effective may or may not be whether a company has plenty of cash. The generation of cash has as much to do with sales volume, operating margins, number of customers, and types of businesses a delivery service deals with, as it has to do with a particular collection program. However, the effectiveness of a specific program can easily be measured in terms of how many days' sales are tied up in accounts receivable, how much of total accounts receivable is current, and what percentage of sales is uncollectible. See page 44 for a method to compute days' sales in accounts receivable.

Our collection program at Mid-Counties resulted in approximately 35 days' sales in accounts receivable, roughly 75 to 80 percent of receivables were less than 30 days old, and our bad debts averaged less than one-half of 1 percent of sales. These were good results.

There is an art to collecting cash. While this activity is not as glamorous as selling and does not receive the same level of attention, without an effective system, poor cash management can make life miserable. ***Cash is King!***

Revenue Forecasts and Budgets | 9 |

Subjects covered in this chapter
- *When companies should prepare budgets*
- *Getting ready for the budget process*
- *Budget forms that are typically used*

S ince the general ledger programs I know best have easy-to-use and easy-to-input budget programs for cost control, I believe all companies should complete budgets annually, with a mid-year update. I am most familiar with the Peachtree and SBC general ledger programs, and know their budget modules work well and are easy to understand and use.

The best way to get the budget information is to have each department manager prepare the budget for his or her own department. While this is a task resisted by almost all sales and operating personnel, it has been my experience that if someone else completes their budget for them, they generally are not committed to the numbers.

Budgeting Procedures

Before managers can begin budgeting the costs for their departments, they need certain information and several forms to be used as worksheets, so when they produce their numbers, the numbers fit into the overall company plan without too much modification.

A month or two before the start of a new calendar or fiscal year, and before the budgeting process can begin, the president needs to meet with the main accounting person (often the controller) and the top sales person.

It is the sales manager's responsibility to come up with a detailed revenue plan for the year, broken down into revenue per month for each type, i.e., on-demand, routes, overnight, second day, freight forwarding, storage, etc. Since sales people, by nature, are very optimistic, the president and the controller should make sure they believe these revenue numbers can be attained before accepting them. Further, as a final incentive, the sales manager's compensation for the year should be tied to attaining those levels of revenue. Typically, the sales manager should have a fairly low salary combined with a commission schedule that kicks in at a low rate as he/she approaches plan and increases as sales targets are met, and if gross margins are attained. Sales people do not like to have any responsibility for gross margins, but it has been my experience that if they are compensated solely on the basis of revenues, they figure out ways to bring in a lot of low-margin business that provides them with high income, while the company struggles to make profits.

The president, with the help of the controller, must establish an overall operating structure that is fair and attainable based on the current operating environment. At Mid-Counties, I usually set the budgets on percentages similar to the following:

Revenues	100%
Expenses:	
Wages and Benefits	50% (Driver wages & benefits = 35%)
Vehicle Costs	15%
Insurance (incl work comp)	10%
Occupancy	4%
Other Costs	13%
Total Expenses	92%
Pretax Income	8%
Taxes	3%
Net Income	5%

There is no reason that a company in this industry should not make more than 5 percent on revenues, but over the years, I found that I was disappointed when I had expectations of higher pretax earnings based on what turned out to be unattained revenues. I found that I was better off if we produced a profit plan that showed revenues on the low side of those forecast by the sales manager, which then led to smaller expense budgets.

After the revenue forecast has been accepted, budget instructions can go out to the department managers with spending guidelines for each department. With the budget instructions, the managers must have the current pay rates for each of their employees, anniversary dates of employment for their employees, a range of acceptable pay increases for their employees, worksheets for use in preparing departmental payroll summaries (including a rate for payroll taxes and benefits that are not budgeted as separate line items), departmental labor distribution worksheets, and finally, the worksheet for the departmental budget. The financial person must allocate certain expenses, such as rent, utilities, insurance, etc., to the various departments and provide this data.

Budget Payroll Summaries

Payroll is ordinarily the most significant expense item for delivery companies, and therefore it takes the most work to come up with proper budget numbers. The budget payroll worksheet lists the employees assigned to each department, with a column for each month's pay plus one more column for that person's total pay for the year (including overtime, bonuses, commissions, etc.). In computing each person's pay for each month, the department manager should figure out how many workdays there are in each month, rather than taking the annual compensation for an employee and dividing that number by twelve. Most months will have different pay amounts since not all have 173 work hours.

Payroll Budget
Department xxx
For 200x

Employee	Jan	Feb	Mar	Apr	May	June	July	Aug	Sept	Oct	Nov	Dec	Total
Porter, G	$1,440	$1,368	$1,656	$1,512	$1,440	$1,584	$1,692	$1,584	$1,512	$1,440	$1,368	$1.425	$18,021
Rogers, D	1,600	1,500	1,800	1,680	1,600	1,760	1,680	1,760	1,630	1,600	1,500	1,550	19,660
Rhoads,S	2,580	2,460	2,900	2,700	2,460	2,820	2,700	2,820	2,700	2,580	2,460	2,695	31,875
P/Rtaxes	955	909	1,087	1,001	935	1,048	1,032	1,048	993	955	909	964	11,836
Total	$6,575	$6,237	$7,443	$6,893	$6,435	$7,212	$7,104	$7,212	$6,835	$6,575	$6,237	$6,634	$81,392

Budget Labor Distribution Summaries

The totals of the payroll summary worksheet for each column are brought forward to the labor distribution worksheet. Here, the totals from the payroll worksheet are shown monthly by the general ledger account to which they are charged. The general ledger accounts for pay are 71001 - 71009 as shown in the chart of accounts beginning on page 21, and the department manager should attempt to break out salaries and wages, vacation pay, bonuses, and commissions.

The labor distribution worksheet should have the same totals as the payroll worksheet.

Labor Distribution Budget
Department xxx
For 200x

Acct#	Jan	Feb	Mar	Apr	May	June	July	Aug	Sept	Oct	Nov	Dec	Total
71001	$6,575	$6,237	$7,443	$6,893	$6,435	$7,212	$6,683	$6,744	$6,835	$6,575	$6,237	$5,669	$79,538
71002												263	263
71005							421	468				702	1,591
Total	$6,575	$6,237	$7,443	$6,893	$6,435	$7,212	$7,104	$7,212	$6,835	$6,575	$6,237	$6,634	$81,392

Budget for Departmental Expenses

The departmental budget begins with the labor distribution brought forward from the labor distribution worksheet, followed by the taxes on those amounts. On Mid-Counties' departmental expense amounts (pages 34 through 38) are shown the types of line items that should be included on each department's budget.

When all anticipated expenses for the year have been included on the worksheet, the sheet should be totaled and the final amount must be equal to or less than the amount approved by the president. If the total is more, then the hard work of cutting costs begins. Once the total amount has been approved, then the details from the budget worksheet are entered into the computer.

It is sometimes easier to skip the budget worksheet and go directly to the budget program in the computer because it foots and cross foots the totals. This can save department managers a lot of time, since most are not very good with an adding machine. If Excel is used for the worksheets, it, of course, sums and cross foots columns.

Expense Budget
Department xxx
For 200x

Acct#	Jan	Feb	Mar	Apr	May	June	July	Aug	Sept	Oct	Nov	Dec	Total
71001	$6,575	$6,237	$7,443	$6,893	$6,435	$7,212	$6,683	$6,744	$6,835	$6,575	$6,237	$5,669	$79,538
71002												263	263
71005							421	468				702	1,591
71111	2,000	2,000	2,000	2,000	2,000	2,000	2,000	2,000	2,000	2,000	2,000	2,000	24,000
71201	600	570	690	630	600	660	630	660	630	600	570	570	7,410
71203	200	200	200	200	200	200	200	200	200	200	200	200	2,400
71204	30	30	30	30	30	30	30	30	30	30	30	30	360
71205			600		500						900		2,000
71207	150	150	150	150	150	150	150	150	150	150	150	150	1,800
71212	20	20	20	20	20	20	20	20	20	20	20	20	240
71301	1,875	1,875	1,875	1,875	1,875	1,875	1,875	1,875	1,875	1,875	1,875	1,875	22,500
71402	45	45	45	45	45	45	45	45	45	45	45	45	540
71501	500	500	500	500	500	500	500	500	500	500	500	500	6,000
Total	$11,995	$11,627	$13,553	$12,343	$12,355	$12,692	$12,554	$12,692	$12,285	$11,995	$12,527	$12,024	$148,642

As indicated above, the budget is usually expected to remain in effect for a full year, but most companies review it after mid-year and often make changes if they find actual revenue is greatly different from plan.

Budget Terminology

A couple of budgeting terms are bandied around by accountants. The first is"**zero-based budgeting.**" This simply means that the budgeter should be prepared to justify every expenditure and amount in his budget. Nothing is sacred, including each employee on his staff. The hope here is that each manager will identify some costs that are no longer necessary to get the job done and will come in with a budget that is under the amount allocated. Zero-based budgeting usually is used for the initial budget of each year.

The second type of budget is called "**percentage**" or "**flexible budgeting.**" This type of budgeting is often used for mid-year or quarterly updates to the zero-based budget produced for the beginning of a year. It applies an approved percentage increase or decrease to the amounts budgeted at the start of the year. Mid-year and quarterly updates are done to keep spending in line with the most current sales results and forecasts.

Large companies usually do an annual budget for **capital asset acquisitions,** too. Although I have not shown a form for this budget, it would be the same as the budget forms shown above, with a column for every month, plus a column for totals. At Mid-Counties I never did capital asset budgeting because our asset purchased were usually small except for the purchase of vehicles, and I could not accurately forecast when we were going to need vehicles. Increases in depreciation expense come from the capital asset budget and if a company does a projected cash flow statement from the budgets, vehicle purchases certainly can have a significant effect on cash.

Enemies in Disguise |10|

Subjects covered in this chapter
- *The horror of workers' compensation*
- *Why payroll services are beneficial*
- *Dealing with the EDD on Unemployment Insurance*

Most people who go into business for themselves understand that they will have to cope with various difficult situations regarding cash flow, competition, employees, etc. However, several other problems, which may not be expected or well understood, can actually be a threat to the very survival of a business.

Workers' Compensation

Possibly the biggest headache and threat to the survival of a business is workers' compensation insurance. This program was established in 1913 as a means of guaranteeing no-fault physical injury insurance to employees hurt on the job, while protecting employers from the risk of lawsuits. Yet, as medical insurance has greatly expanded and the number of persons working in dangerous factories has diminished, workers' comp rates have increased rather than fallen, and injuries have risen as employment has become safer.

The premiums for workers' comp insurance are paid 100 percent by employers (businesses, school districts, cities, and counties). Certain large business are allowed self-funding and do not pay premiums, but small and mid-sized businesses that have employees must all be covered by the plan and pay its premiums.

Aside from the employers who pay the workers' comp premiums and the employees who receive the benefits, other parties interested in the program are insurers, lawyers, labor unions, doctors and chiropractors. I have read that in California alone, workers' comp premiums are $20 billion a year and increasing. Because this pool of money is so large, persons in each of the interest groups would like to get their hands on some of it. Fraud in the program is enormous.

To get an idea of the cost to a delivery business to fund workers' comp, the average California business pays about 5 percent of its employees' pay as workers' comp premiums. However, a delivery company now pays 20 to 25 percent of its driver's wages as workers' comp premiums. This means that for a $15 dollar an hour driver ($31,200 per year with no overtime), the annual workers' comp premium will be around $7,500. Drivers that work for other types of companies such as insurance or bakeries have lower workers' comp premiums. Construction employees such as carpenters have higher rates and can be rated for workers' compensation purposes at 100 percent or more of the employee's pay.

Workers' compensation premiums are set by employee classification within industries by a Rating Bureau. It is my understanding that the insurance companies fund this rating bureau, so you can see where the loyalties for this group reside. In California, the Department of Industrial Relations oversees the workers' comp program and a person whose prior work experience has all been in union organization heads this department. Also in California, there is an elected insurance commissioner whose job it is to make sure that the citizens of the state are well served by the providers of the insurance. However, this system has meant that Republican commissioners (such as Commissioner Quackenbush, who was forced out of office for not performing his duties, as well as diverting insurance funds into his personal re-election accounts) are biased in favor of the insurance companies and Democratic commissioners are biased in favor of employees. No person or organization in the workers' compensation system cares a whit about the employers who fund the system.

A specific company's rates are adjusted by a modification factor worked up by the Rating Bureau, based on the company's workers' compensation claims during three of the last four years. The lowest mod factor I ever heard of was 65 percent, and my guess is that even if a company had no claims during its three-year period, it would never be given a mod factor lower than 65 percent. Some delivery companies have had mod factors of 100 percent or more. For every dollar of wages, they pay a dollar to the insurance industry for this coverage.

All delivery companies are required by law to carry workers' compensation insurance on all employees (except, in most cases, on owners). However, a major problem exists in that many insurance companies do not want to write workers' compensation on delivery companies. The way the system works is that an agent of the insurance company obtains information about the delivery company, including an estimate of its payrolls for the coming twelve months. If the payroll estimate is small or if the company has had a number of claims during the last four years, no insurance company will bid on this account. If no insurance company wants to carry it, then the State Fund must carry it. As you would expect, the State Fund is usually not a low cost workers' compensation carrier. In order to obtain coverage, the insurance carrier might force a delivery company to use a higher estimate of payroll for the coming year or even to change its classification to an industry with higher rates so the insurance company will make more money.

When a quote from an insurance carrier is selected by the delivery company, the company is required to pay all or a down payment of 10 to 30 percent of the estimated annual premiums; the insurance company or a finance company carries the balance, with principal and interest payments made monthly, usually over seven or eight months. Even though workers' comp is based on employees' pay over the coming year, it must be paid in advance, well before employees actually work (and are exposed to injury, or are paid).

After the down payment, which binds the contract, monthly payments of the remainder of the annual premium begin. There are two types of policies for monthly payments. One is called a reporting policy. Under this method, the actual employee's pay for the previous month is reported to the insurance company by workers' comp classification (*drivers* [highest rates], *outside sales,* or *clerical* for delivery companies), and the insurance company sends the delivery company a bill for the next month's premium, adjusted by the delivery company's mod factor. The other policy is a flat monthly payment based on the delivery company's estimate at the start of the policy year.

Any employee whose job description does not fall into the above three classifications must be included in the classification with the highest rate. When my daughter was in college, I had her come in every week and do the janitorial work in our office. I was required to pay workers' compensation on her as if she were a driver. The workers' comp auditors also like to put a company's highest paid managers into the driver category because this really drives up the cost.

After the end of the policy year, an insurance auditor visits the company and computes the earned premiums based on the delivery company's payrolls. If there is a difference between the auditor's calculations and the company's payments, the company soon receives an invoice for any premium shortage; if the premiums were overpaid, the company should theoretically receive a refund. As you might expect, refunds are very difficult to collect and often are never paid. On the other hand, additional monies owed the insurance company are billed promptly and if not paid promptly are turned over to a collection agency.

In order to obtain any workers' compensation business, the state insurance commissioner must approve an insurance company. Once approved, its rates are posted and agents submit requests from companies seeking coverage to the carrier. The carrier is eligible to write as much or as little of the workers' comp market as it wants. Because of this system, workers' compensation insurance companies understand that they have only one customer, and that customer is the state. They have no regard for or interest in the companies they insure. Their claims processing is usually outsourced to another company that handles claims for a number of insurance companies; problems and disputes about premiums, payments and coverage are handled by the agents; and therefore there is usually no contact between the insurance company and the employer. There certainly is no "customer-vendor" relationship, and an employer never builds loyalty from an insurance company, no matter how long the employer has paid premiums to a particular company. An insurance company can replace the premiums paid by one small business with the premiums of 100 more waiting in the shadows just hoping to get away from the State Fund.

An insurance company can easily prosper under this program. A few years ago, a wealthy race horse owner from San Diego was having a problem obtaining insurance (including workers' comp) for his horse racing activities, so he formed a company named Golden Eagle Insurance to provide insurance for his own activities. However, after Golden Eagle was approved by the California Insurance Commissioner, this person (his name was John Maybe) began accepting workers' compensation insurance from companies in various industries around the state. He was very interested in the courier and trucking industries and offered companies in these industries rebates on their workers' compinsation costs if they had few or no claims when covered by Golden Eagle.

Golden Eagle became a multimillion-dollar company almost overnight. It operated out of what looked like an old motel in Southern California and had very few employees. The story was that John Maybe began to take loans from Golden Eagle that soon totaled over $1 million, with no intent to repay. Golden Eagle also paid very few of the rebates it had promised its policyholders. After being in business for five or six years, California Insurance Commissioner Quackenbush took over the operations from Mr. Maybe, ostensibly because of the unpaid loans. (Maybe maintained that Quackenbush took over Golden Eagle because he had refused to contribute to a re-election fund for Quackenbush.) Golden Eagle was sold to one of the other large workers' compensation companies for millions that went to Maybe (and it appears that Maybe was able to keep the loans he had made to himself). Every dollar of this money came from the employers in California.

I had firsthand knowledge of this situation—I had moved my company's workers' compensation coverage to Golden Eagle because of the rebate program. I earned nice rebates over the three years I was insured by them, but they refused to pay them. When I complained to Commissioner Quackenbush, he turned my complaint over to the Rating Bureau, and with no investigation, the Rating Bureau promptly sided with Golden Eagle. I had to take Golden Eagle to court to collect my rebates. I easily won my case, but the legal fees ate up most of the rebates I received.

In my experience, many employees are convinced they themselves pay a portion or all of the workers' compensation premiums. They then look at it as part of their medical coverage and attempt to have every cold, flu, and minor illness become work related. At Mid-Counties, we were successful in managing our workers' comp mod factor by having the company pay for all first aid types of injuries and by not running these nicks and scratches through workers' compensation. By using this method, we were able to keep our mod factor between 65 and 70 percent over many years. The only problems we faced were from the few employees who demanded to use workers' compensation to see a doctor just because it was their right, and who used doctors that would rather deal with the workers' compensation system than with an employer. These doctors scheduled many follow-up appointments, rather than treat a person once for a minor problem. When doctor visits go through the workers' compensation system, doctors can schedule months of follow-up treatments, whereas an employer, of course, does not want these appointments to go on and on, especially when the employee says he is well. I recently read that in California, injured employees that go to chiropractors average 34 visits before they are released.

The real problem with workers' compensation is that it takes employer's money that could go to worthwhile employee programs such as medical benefits or higher pay and funnels it into the insurance industry. Employers and most employees get almost no benefit from workers' compensation. Employees would be much better off if workers' compensation were combined with the regular medical coverage most companies now provide. A major medical override could be written to cover catastrophic injuries, although these seem to be rare these days, so the cost of the major medical coverage should be very cheap. I believe that such a combination of the two insurance programs could provide medical coverage to millions of workers not now covered and could at the same time reduce insurance costs to all businesses. Of course, doctors and unions are dead-set against such a combination.

An interesting fact is that, as far as I know, no other country in the world has evolved a program whereby businesses are primarily responsible for paying for workers' medical insurance. Since medical insurance currently costs somewhere around $600 - $1,000 a month (or more) for an employee and his dependants and is going up dramatically every year, anyone thinking of going into business for themselves where their revenues are directly related to the number of employees they have should think long and hard about assuming this incredible burden. As you may know, Wal-Mart, McDonald's and many other large, international companies have historically not paid for health insurance for their rank and file workers. This appears to be changing, at least in California, because of legislation recently on the ballot. It is probably just a matter of time before one of these initiatives becomes law and workers' compensation and health insurance premiums for a $10 an hour married employee amount to $2,500 a month. Said another way, health insurance and workers' compensation premiums could easily cost $30,000 a year for an employee who earns $20,800. These high benefit costs certainly limit the potential for operating a successful small business.

The Internal Revenue Service

The primary exposure to serious problems with the IRS occurs when mistakes are made with payroll withholdings. The prompt, accurate payment of withheld payroll taxes is so critical that thousands of payroll services can be found throughout the country to take care of payroll processing, tax calculation and payment, in spite of the fact that every general ledger software program has an inexpensive payroll module that can compute these payments and indicate the payroll tax due dates.

I had a horrible experience with the IRS about 10 years ago when they lost a large payroll tax payment of Mid-Counties and were never able to find it. After much correspondence, we sent a replacement check through the mail. The IRS again said they could not find it, and it was not until a second replacement check was sent to a specific person in their Fresno processing location that the payment was received.

Between the mailing of the second and third remittances, we were visited by IRS agents who walked around our facilities showing pistols strapped under their arms. It was a very frightening situation. Other than again making payments that I had already made, there was nothing I could do to placate them. Fortunately, we had some dealings with the SBA, and the SBA was able to contact IRS personnel at a much higher level and work out the logistics of our third remittance. Without the SBA's intervention, I believe my company would have been shut down and the doors padlocked.

After this episode, I switched payroll services to one that made the payroll tax payments for us.

I do not think it is good business for any small company to prepare its own payroll and handle its own payroll tax calculations and payments. The penalties for late payment of payroll taxes are very high, but the costs to use a payroll service are low. In addition, this is one of those rare situations where the government can go after the officers of a business to get withheld funds. I know of several situations where business owners were forced to sell their homes to obtain funds to satisfy the IRS.

Unemployment Claims

Another social program that can become very costly to a company is unemployment insurance. This program, like workers' comp and payroll taxes, is based on what is typically the largest expense a company incurs, employee pay. Even small increases in payroll ripple through these related costs to take a big bite out of profits.

During the 15 years I was in business, I made every effort to keep unemployment taxes at a minimum by reducing employee turnover. I did this by paying higher than market wages, continually working with marginal employees, spending extra time on training, providing good benefits, being flexible on time off, hiring relatives of employees, paying bonuses, etc. These programs were successful to the extent that the company developed a nice $50,000 unemployment reserve and earned an ever-improving U.I. payroll rate of about 1.5 percent. However, in spite of my attempts to control charges to the unemployment reserve account, employees who left the company for any reason were always able to obtain full unemployment pay. This was very frustrating to me, especially in the cases where employees were discharged for cause.

Based on my experience in dealing with the EDD, I believe there are virtually no conditions under which an employee will not receive unemployment pay. I have contested awards to employees for the following reasons and always lost:

- Employee discharged for excessive absenteeism or tardiness
- Employee discharged for rudeness to customers
- Employee discharged for purposeful damage to freight
- Employee discharged because of too many driving tickets and company unable to obtain insurance on driver
- Employee discharged because of numerous accidents over several months
- Employee quit to take higher paying job over 100 miles away
- Employee quit to go to school
- Employee quit to take care of sick friend
- Employee refused to come to work

Although I have contested hundreds of unemployment awards over the years and have gone before administrative appeals judges on many cases, as far as I can remember, I have never won a single case. I have even lost cases where the employee failed to show up for the meeting with the judge. I am convinced that numerous administrative law judges over long careers have never once found in favor of an employer. I believe these judges are employed as window dressing to provide the appearance of a fair and just system.

This has led me to conclude that unemployment insurance is a program that employers have no control over other than to decide when an employee should be discharged. Employers simply provide the monies to the EDD so benefits can be paid to whomever applies for them. An employer must pay for unemployment insurance while an employee is on his payroll and then continue to pay by having the company's reserve account charged after the employee leaves. Federal and state auditors regularly visit to make sure companies pay the amounts auditors determine. However, there are no agencies, groups or commissioners to look out for employer rights because employers have no rights other than the right to contest and lose.

Summary

The money to run our government comes mainly from citizens and businesses. Citizens can get their needs met by many means, but their most powerful tool is their ability to vote for politicians that support their ideals. Large businesses can hire lobbyists and make meaningful campaign contributions to promote their programs and success. Small businesses contribute mightily to employee programs and to the well-being of the country, but have almost no say in the development of these and other national programs. As these programs become increasingly burdensome, small businesses are left to their own devices to figure out how to cope and stay alive.

Currently, small businesses are making a major movement to outsource all jobs previously handled by employees. The major corporations began this process years ago, and now there are no tanneries or textile companies in the U.S., footwear is just about gone, most steel mills are shut down, chemicals appear to be moving off-shore, and semiconductor manufacturing lines and even software are rapidly leaving the U.S. Before long, the only jobs available in the U.S. will be low paying service jobs and jobs with the government.

Delivery businesses have few options when attempting to cut costs. By far the largest cost for a delivery service is its payroll and related payroll taxes and benefits. Many delivery services have been managing these costs over the last few years by reclassifying their drivers from employees to independent contractors and in some cases then transferring the contractors to a temporary help company that leases them back to the delivery company.

If a company is convinced that it can meet the IRS and EDD qualifying rules to reclassify employees to independent contractors (see page 78), it generally can avoid the following employer obligations.

- Workers' compensation is not provided.
- Disability insurance, life insurance, sick pay and vacation pay is not provided.
- Income tax withholding, unemployment insurance wthholding and benefits, state disability insurance, paid family leave, employment training tax, Social Security withholding and payment, and Medicare are not provided.
- Medical insurance and retirement are not provided.
- Wage and hour laws which include minimum wage, overtime, and rest periods do not apply.
- Anti-discrimination rules involving race, sex, national origin, age, disability, ancestry, religion, etc. do not apply.
- Return to work obligations under disability laws do not apply.
- Wrongful employment termination and related causes of action do not apply.

As you might expect, the delivery companies I know that have been able to justify this reclassification have become more profitable and have been able to reduce their delivery prices and obtain a lion's share of new business as it becomes available.

Selling a Delivery Service | 11 |

Subjects covered in this chapter
- *Who buys delivery companies*
- *Tax and accounting considerations*
- *Tips to help the seller realize the sales price*

Most small businesses are a real problem to sell. They often are too little to interest a large company, and yet they can be too big for most individuals to buy. The sale of a delivery service can be an even larger problem because few businesses in the industry can afford to buy another. Unless the seller has a strategic location, an especially attractive list of customers, or a unique service or two, few want or can afford his company. In order to make a purchase attractive, most sellers must offer very lenient terms.

The Way Delivery Companies Are Often Sold

Historically, many delivery companies have been liquidated and dissolved, or at best, they were sold to another company for a small down payment supplemented by a 6 to 10 percent commission on collected sales over some period such as 36 months. With this type of purchase, the buyer has almost no commitment to make the sale successful. And with this type of payment arrangement, the seller can count on the buyer's losing most of the seller's former business, so the commissions often do not amount to much.

When I sold Mid-Counties Delivery Service, I contacted some of the largest delivery services in the same metropolitan area with services at least partially similar to mine. Since we also had a rapidly growing international freight forwarding division and potential purchasers wanted to get into that business, it was not too difficult to get interest in acquiring the company from almost all of them. The problem, as always, was to get a fair price for what I had built. In retrospect, I wish I had sent a notice of my desire to sell to all the couriers and delivery companies in the California Delivery Association. By contacting only a few companies well known to me, I am sure I limited the range of offers I received.

In the end, I sold for a small down payment (that really represented the fair market value of my vehicles) and an 8 percent commission on collected sales to my customers over a 36-month period. I kept my receivables and payables because the buyers wanted to charge back any receivables over a certain age and I did not believe they would make an honest attempt to collect them.

When evaluating the final three potential acquirers, I found them to be similar in several important respects. They were all weak financially and were having trouble making money at the time of the sale. Even though their annual revenues ranged from $2.5 million to over $10 million, they made remarkably similar offers — no down payment or a low down payment and commissions at the rates of 8 to 10 percent over three years. (I believe these three firms all used the same accountant for their financial counseling and taxes.) Any of these offers would have been very lucrative had the buyer been able to hold my business and continue to experience the growth rates I did.

It took almost a year and a half from the time I had a statement of intent from the first serious buyer until a deal was closed (a third potential buyer thrust his company into the mix at the ninth hour). During this period, I got to know the managements of the companies fairly well. I found that even the largest of the potential buyers was very unsophisticated financially, even though the company had a large financial staff. The buyers seemed obsessed with the idea of getting rid of Mid-Counties' employees, including my drivers. They all seemed disinterested with the concept of gross margin on sales. I spent a lot of time trying to show them that my business would pay for itself in a matter of months if they could just keep my accounts and maintain my prices. I tried to convince them that they were acquiring my gross margins, which is much better and more important than acquiring just the customer list and revenues. But none of the potential buyers bought into this concept; I believe they did not understand it.

When I selected the buyer, one of my main concerns was to make sure my prices were at least as high as the buyer's, so he would not have to jack my rates up to meet his way of doing business, and by so doing drive my customers away.

As I talked to the potential buyers, they all instigated a lot of discussion about on-time delivery percentages. They all professed to have on-time deliveries of about 99 percent, and I was ashamed to tell them that I did not track on-time deliveries any more, since we almost never lost a customer because of poor service. When for some reason we did miss a delivery, we always downgraded our charge to the appropriate lower rate and our customers seemed reasonably happy with this program. Unfortunately, after I sold my company it turned out that these on-time delivery statistics were either untrue or meaningless, and the new buyer began losing my old customers immediately because of poor service. He could not even make pickups on time, let alone deliveries. My best customers began to leave shortly after the sale, and by the end of the first year, most of the significant accounts were gone. Although some customers left to go with small competitors, most of the good customers went to former employees of Mid-Counties, even though we had non-compete agreements with most of them. I believe many customers migrate away from a new buyer to former employees because they associate the former employee with the old business.

I ran up large legal fees protecting my old customers from several former employees, but the real issue to me was why someone would buy my customers, some of whom had been with me for 10 to 15 years, and then provide such rotten service that the customers left.

Since an owner selling a company in this industry does not have many options, if he decides that selling the business based on some future commission is the best deal he can get, he should attempt to incorporate the following provisions in the agreement.

The down payment should be at least the fair market value of any assets transferred to the buyer. While it is usually easy to get the buyer to pay blue book for vehicles, the seller should also negotiate a value for supplies, forms, and fully depreciated assets such as printers and computers, and list these items and prices in the sales agreement. After the sale, I found that these items plus even pencils, chairs and file cabinets were very important to the buyer. In retrospect, he obtained more benefit from these items than from some of my biggest customers that he could not keep.

As you may know, it is difficult to sell software these days, unless it is home made. The software companies, as a rule, do not allow the transfer of title to a purchaser of a business. However, the software used by a business affords enormous value to the buyer since it lets him view the rating algorithms, the makeup of the rate sheet, customer details, customer usage levels, details of billings, accounts receivable, cash applications, revenues by pickup or delivery location, etc. In my situation, the buyer was acquiring international freight forwarding and remail services that he knew little about, and he needed the information in the computer to help him understand that part of the business.

Contractually I was unable to transfer title of the software to the buyer, and he refused to pay for its use. But, as he began to fold the Mid-Counties business into his company, he began to see how important that information was. He took a file server that held the programs to his main location, although after moving the computer he was not able access many of the files. The point is that if he had been willing to pay for my information and had sought my assistance in the migration, he would have had a far easier time integrating my business into his, and would have saved a lot of money. As it was, it took him over 60 days to get to the point where he could begin to bill my customers (and it probably took him another 60 days to collect those charges because the invoices were so late). This is all part of the greater problem associated with buying a business for the absolute minimum amount. These types of purchases do not recognize the value of any part of the seller's business other than the customers. In addition to buying too few assets, the buyers take far too few employees, especially operations and customer service personnel. Without these important employees, the buyer quickly loses the flavor of the purchased business. He then often attempts to vacate the seller's premises in order to save some more money and to service the area remotely. These actions will always contribute to terrible customer service and unhappy customers.

In my opinion, sales of companies handled in this manner are bad for both the buyer and the seller. I estimate that low-down-payment, commission-based business purchases are successful in retaining only about 25 to 35 percent of the selling company's accounts. I contrast this to 15 years earlier when I purchased Mid-Counties and took all of the seller's assets (except cash and accounts receivable-payable) and all of their employees. As far as I know, we lost no accounts, and certainly no significant customers.

> **The following information is provided as general information only and is not meant to suggest tax or accounting treatment for a specific purchase or sale. The information is in summary form and does not present the entire spectrum of the various accounting and tax possibilities. A business purchaser or seller should seek advice from its own attorney and outside accountant for the most current tax and accounting regulations.**

Ways of Structuring a Sale

Businesses in other industries are not usually sold with low down payments followed by several years of monthly commissions on collected revenues of the sold business. Certainly, businesses that have high-value assets are not sold this way. Since there are hundreds of books about various structures for the sale of businesses, and since practically all public accounting firms and legal firms have specialists who are experts in the most current tax and accounting treatment of these transactions, I will not go into much detail on these more typical sales agreements. They are very common outside the transportation industry and occur in the transportation industry when a sales agent or broker is involved. The valuation of a service business is ordinarily some multiple of pretax profits or cash flow increased by interest, depreciation and amortization, and owner's expenses (draw or salary, bonuses, vehicle expenses, insurance, medical benefits, retirement, etc.), The multiple for a service business is often in the range of three to five times the adjusted annual pretax profit, or three to five times the annual free cash flow. When a service business is growing rapidly or has a special niche, but is not very profitable, the company can be valued on the basis of a certain number of month's sales—again as much as three to five.

Since most companies are corporations because of the legal protection afforded, the simplest way to buy one is to buy its stock. A company may be acquired by buying its stock with cash or with the acquiring company's stock. In general, a stock-for-cash acquisition is called a purchase; a stock-for-stock acquisition is called a merger. If the buyer pays a premium for the stock over its net book value—assets less liabilities—the premium is usually recorded as goodwill. All other assets and liabilities remain the same. Goodwill is a strange asset, since it is amortized for tax purposes over a very long period, like 15 years. For book purposes, goodwill is written off faster or slower depending on the perceived worth of the acquired company in subsequent years. If, for example, the buyer loses most of the accounts of the acquired company, the goodwill should be written down as the customers leave.

Mergers

A stock-for-stock acquisition is especially common when the stock of the acquiring company is publicly traded. This type of transaction is called a merger as opposed to a purchase, and it has certain specific tax and legal ramifications. One of the most important is that the selling shareholders do not incur any income tax liability on the sale (merger) of their business until they dispose of the shares they received from the buying company. Another ramification is that when a person or company buys the stock of a corporation, the buyer is responsible for the debts of the company acquired; this can include lawsuits or other significant unrecorded liabilities.

During the dot.com boom, many companies went public with few or no revenues and saw their stock valuations go sky-high. They then began to use this highly valued stock to purchase other dot.com companies at high values (no cash changed hands). This is why, when the stock market bubble burst, quarterly earnings reports for these dot.com companies reported practically no revenues and yet showed millions or billions of dollars in losses. The companies were writing off goodwill recorded when they bought companies with their stock at exorbitant values.

Stock-for-stock mergers in the delivery industry are extremely rare because the buyers are usually small, private companies, and there is usually no market for their stock—so the seller does not want it.

Purchases

In a stock-for-cash purchase of a company, the transaction will usually result in a gain or loss to the sellers for tax purposes. Under this type of acquisition, the buyer is responsible for all debts of the acquired company, whether or not they were disclosed or known at the date of purchase. Certain other attributes of a company—such as a tax loss carry forward, worker's compensation mod factor, trade names, and all legal rights and obligations—are transferred to the new owner along with the stock he bought.

Acquiring Only Certain Assets of a Business

For several reasons, many buyers are not willing to assume the risk that all liabilities are disclosed and known, or that the seller's books have been properly recorded. They, therefore, buy only certain assets of a company, leaving the corporate structure with the sellers to later be liquidated. This frees the buyer of all or any of the seller's liabilities.

With this type of purchase, the buyer is free to revalue the assets purchased to their current market value, since the seller would have recorded these assets at historical cost. Also, it would be unlikely that the seller would have recorded as assets certain intangible assets such as customer lists, business names, contact names, internet sites and names, homemade software application programs, specialized know-how, telephone and fax numbers, etc. But a buyer could assign value to these assets, record them on the company's books and amortize them over some reasonable period. Again, any amount paid that was not allocated to specific assets would be recorded as goodwill.

Unless the capital stock of a company is acquired, any cash on the company's books usually stays with the seller. And since the accounts payable and other liabilities of a company are often not assumed by the buyer, the seller may have to retain his accounts receivable in order to get enough cash to pay his payables.

Potential Problems for Sellers of Delivery Businesses

Since most small businesses in this industry are sold for commissions for a certain number of months on business that is retained, the seller should anticipate the following issues that may arise.

Income statements, measurement of company size, many loan applications, most credit ratings, company growth, governmental groupings of companies by industry or for consensus purposes, etc., are based on revenues. One would expect, therefore, that revenues would be the primary basis for calculating commissions for the purchase of a business. Not so! A buyer from within the industry will not be satisfied with a commission payment based on sales, but instead will want to pay commissions only on the cash received from the collections of the sales. If the seller has had few bad debts over the years, he might not consider this a significant issue. But this can become a very big issue and a major headache for the seller. The seller may think he would be satisfied with receiving a commission check each month based on the collection of receivables, but unless contractually prohibited, this opens the door to "unusual" accounting practices by the buyer.

The buyer might want to increase the pace of his collections by offering a cash discount of as much as two percent to customers who pay within a few days of the billing. This, of course, would reduce the cash collections and decrease the amount of commissions to the seller. Cash discounts for early payment of receivables should be covered in the contract.

Some transportation companies are in the habit of offsetting receivables and payables instead of writing checks. For example, if one of the seller's customers is a law firm, the buyer might want to swap court filings for legal services. This type of barter would decrease cash collections and affect the amount of commissions the seller would receive. Offsetting in general should not be allowed per stipulation in the contract.

Another action that will reduce accounts receivable and cash collections is the issuance of credit memos. The seller should contractually be able to approve or disapprove credit memos over a certain amount to his former customers. If he does not approve a specific credit memo, it should not affect his commissions. For example, if the buyer makes an air shipment for one of the seller's former customers, the freight is damaged in transit, and the buyer issues a credit memo, this should be the buyer's problem and the credit memo should not decrease the seller's commissions on that shipment.

The seller will have little control over the buyer's collection activities. The seller may believe he could collect accounts that the buyer ignores and in due course writes off. For this reason, the seller should negotiate a fair, fixed bad debt rate or amount, based on his own experience with these accounts. If actual write-offs exceed this number, they should not affect the commission payments.

While most businesses are interested in keeping sales prices and revenues as high as possible, a buyer might feel compelled to offer certain discounts and allowances that result in lower sales prices and lower sales than the seller previously charged his customers. Discounts or allowances, for whatever reason, should be covered in the sales agreement and generally should be prohibited, unless approved by the seller.

Some buyers want to exclude receivables over 60 or 90 days old from commission payments, even if the old balances are partially or fully collected later. This provision can be particularly important at the end of the contract period, because if the buyer stops collection activities near the end of the contract, 60 or 90 days after the end of the contract the seller would not be entitled to any more commissions even if cash collections were significant.

I believe that even if a contract is signed that pays a seller a commission based on cash collections, there should be some guaranteed minimum monthly payment that protects the seller from gross mismanagement by the buyer. For example, if a business has been operating at an annual sales level of $1,000,000 for a few years and is sold for an 8 percent commission payable monthly over three years, the seller would expect a monthly check of around $7,000. In this case, the seller should bargain for a guaranteed minimum monthly payment of $1,500 to $2,500 (25 to 40 percent of expected commissions) to protect his revenue stream from mismanagement by the buyer, lack of support by the buyer, changes in the economy, environmental factors, governmental regulations, acts of God, etc.

Because the buyer will maintain all of the accounting records after the purchase, it would be easy for him to reduce his monthly commission payments purposefully or in error by not reporting certain sales or collections. It is imperative, therefore, that the seller receive detailed schedules that show the calculation of the monthly commission payments. Ideally, the schedules should show collections or sales by invoice number by customer, multiplied by the commission rate to equal the payment. Summary schedules by customer are not adequate because they can hide adjustments and credits.

The seller should have the right to audit the buyer's records (sales registers, cash receipts journals, and aged accounts receivable trial balances) every six months should he have serious reservations about the propriety of the payments to him.

The timing of the recording of revenues and receivables is very important to the seller. In the delivery business, and especially for same day deliveries, it is important for sales agreement purposes that work is recorded the day it begins (the pickup), not the day the delivery is made—if it is different. And certainly not the date the buyer prepares his invoices. In my situation, the buyer initially put off billing my customers for two months and took several months longer to collect these late billings. I had not anticipated this, so I had no provision in the contract to cover the situation.

The seller should make sure his customers are spelled out specifically in the agreement. If this is not done, the seller may later find out that the two companies have a number of customers in common. If so, the buyer will probably resist paying commissions on the common accounts.

Finally, keep in mind that the buyer is in control, since he maintains the records and writes the checks. Any questions about payments of commissions that are not spelled out in the contract will automatically be decided in favor of the buyer by the buyer, unless the seller elects to get an attorney involved. And at $300 to $500 an hour, using an attorney to resolve a dispute should be the last resort.

A sale to Someone From Outside the Industry

Most delivery businesses are sold to competitors or other delivery companies that want to establish a foothold in the seller's service area. But there is also an opportunity to sell to a buyer from outside the industry if the company is well run and shows steady growth and profits. This type of sale is somewhat different from selling to knowledgeable persons from within the industry.

The business must be marketed differently, much like selling a house. The seller should probably retain an agent or business broker and prepare detailed historical information as well as forecasts. The potential buyer in all likelihood will have little knowledge of the industry or the company for sale.

In addition to the agent's sales channels, the seller must consider other ways of listing the company, such as local newspapers, "The Wall Street Journal," and even Internet services such as eBay

The seller should be prepared to provide some financial help to the buyer, such as extended payment terms, but even so, it is difficult to find a person or small team of buyers that could purchase a company as large as $1,000,000 in revenues.

An eligible buyer is usually willing to pay a higher price for a solid delivery company than would someone from the same industry. Industry insiders would probably expect to pay somewhere around $250,000 over three years for a $1 million dollar company—all based on collections of accounts receivable. Outsiders would probably pay as much as $500,000 and they would be more likely to pay a fixed amount for the business, plus interest at a low rate on the amount financed by the owner.

Even though a sale to a person or an entity outside the transportation industry is a long shot, it certainly bears investigating if a company has a good track record and can stand up to the scrutiny such a sale involves.

Pros and Cons of the Delivery Industry | 12 |

Subjects covered in this chapter
- *Negative aspects of ownership unique to this industry*
- *Nice things about the delivery industry*

At various times before I bought Mid-Counties Delivery Service, I owned several apartment buildings as well as a small ski shop. I thought the ownership of these businesses combined with the experiences I had as a senior manager at several high tech companies provided the background for me to easily manage a small delivery business. While this was true to a certain extent, there were, however, several difficult aspects of the delivery industry that I had not anticipated.

Negative Aspects of this Type of Business

The time sensitive nature of on-demand same day deliveries puts management in a hot seat from the time the first order is received each morning until the last driver goes home in the evening. Customers use on-demand services to receive materials and information that are very important to them; and, therefore, they have little tolerance for deliveries that are almost late. Most customers really expect a 2 hour delivery to be made in 1-1/2 hours. Customers not only become upset when deliveries are not made early, they can become just as irate if pickups are not made shortly after the order is placed. If a customer orders a 2 hour delivery and the pickup is made an hour after the order is placed, most customers will be on the phone to find out why the package was not picked up right after the order was placed. In the mind of the customer, the slow pickup increases the likelihood of a late delivery. Many customers begin calling about half an hour before a delivery is due to get assurance that the package is nearby. This constant questioning and second-guessing is why operations personnel in this industry need to be thick skinned. They often must take a lot of verbal abuse from customers. It seems that on some days when traffic is a mess, or when a number of drivers do not show up, an aura of tension permeates the entire company, and everyone is affected.

Another difficult aspect of this business for me was the ever-present potential for a serious vehicle accident. Fortunately, during the fifteen years that I owned Mid-Counties, our vehicles were never involved in accidents where people were seriously injured. However, that possibility was always in the back of my mind and I shuddered every time I learned that one of our drivers was involved in an accident. It seems to me that we were involved in many more accidents when we drove small vehicles. For whatever reasons, our large trucks were involved in fewer accidents, and the accidents in which we were involved were not major.

I also worried about too many small accidents, which could mean that we would be unable to obtain vehicle and liability insurance. Of course, without insurance, we would be shut down.

A final area of the delivery business that I found to be a problem was my perception that some of our customers seemed to have little loyalty to us, even after a number of years of excellent service. When a new manager became our contact in a company where we had a long and successful relationship, we often had to start from scratch to re-justify our position. I attribute this lack of loyalty to a great extent on the intense competition in the delivery industry; although, I also believe most transportation managers have little understanding of the intricacies and complexities of the same day delivery business. They apparently believe there is little difference between companies in this industry. It was a source of great pride to me, when, after we a lost a good account to an aggressive competitor, we were called back to the company because our service was so much better than the company that had replaced us.

Positive Aspects of this Type of Business

Capital to purchase vehicles and thereby increase revenues is very easy to obtain in this industry. Whereas banks and leasing companies can be very difficult to deal with when seeking expansion capital, I found that the truck and van manufacturers were always ready to sell me up to 5 vehicles at a time with almost no cash down and little in the way of credit verification. This meant that whenever we were able to obtain new business, we had no trouble obtaining the assets with which to make deliveries for our new customers. This is a very positive attribute of this type of business that is not found in most industries.

Another positive feature of this industry is a readily available and inexpensive workforce that can be trained in a relatively short period. For a time when we needed drivers, we had to stop advertising in the local newspaper because we got so many applicants there was not enough room in our office for them to come inside and fill out application forms. Also, while most of the more glamorous industries, such as high-tech, have an aversion to older employees, we found that drivers in their 60's, 70's and even 80's made marvelous employees. And we sought them out.

The delivery business is a "clean industry" and does not require a myriad of permits or filings with the local, state and federal governments. Also, there are no inventories to produce, manage and pay taxes on; there are no sales taxes to collect, report and pay; and because vehicles generally constitute the largest physical asset class and the taxes on them are paid as license renewal fees, property taxes for delivery services are low. And finally, this industry serves a very broad market. Almost every business has a regular need for urgent deliveries.

It has been several years since I sold Mid-Counties Delivery Service and not a day goes by that I do not think of some pleasant aspect of my involvement there. Now that I have closed out a long business career, I find that my time spent in the delivery industry resulted in some of the most satisfying experiences I had in a multitude of diverse jobs.

Index

About the Author

James M. Hansell MBA, CPA Graduated from the University of Denver with a BSBA in Accounting followed by an MBA. He spent seven years on the audit staff of the San Francisco office of Price Waterhouse & Co. where he worked with some of the firm's largest and most successful clients. He also helped form the office's small business group where he reviewed business and financial systems for many small businesses. He spent the next 20 years in senior financial positions as controller or vice president finance in the Silicon Valley high tech industry in a handful of companies, large and small, public and private. In 1988 he purchased a small delivery service in the San Francisco bay area and managed and grew that company until 2002 when he sold it and retired.

Order Form

This book may be ordered with this form or on our website.

Name ————————————————————————————

Address ——————————————————————————

City, State, Zip ————————————————————————

Please send me:

————— copies of *The Business of Same Day Deliveries* at $47.50 $ ————

Shipping: $4.00 first copy and $2.00 for each additional copy $ ————

California residents please add sales tax at - $3.90 each $ ————

Total enclosed $ ————

Payment must accompany order and can be made by check or moany order. Credit card orders may be placed at our website: www.mcdpublishing.com. Allow 3 weeks for delivery.

Send orders to:

MCD Publishing
P.O. Box 330
Santa Clara, CA 95052
Tel: (408) 244-7006
Fax: (408) 244-3757